Business
Communication

The Harvard Business Essentials Series

The Harvard Business Essentials series is designed to provide comprehensive advice, personal coaching, background information, and guidance on the most relevant topics in business. Drawing on rich content from Harvard Business School Publishing and other sources, these concise guides are carefully crafted to provide a highly practical resource for readers with all levels of experience. To assure quality and accuracy, each volume is closely reviewed by a specialized content adviser from a world-class business school. Whether you are a new manager interested in expanding your skills or an experienced executive looking for a personal resource, these solution-oriented books offer reliable answers at your fingertips.

Other books in the series:

Finance for Managers
Hiring and Keeping the Best People
Managing Change and Transition
Negotiation
Managing Creativity and Innovation

Business Communication

Harvard Business School Press | *Boston, Massachusetts*

Copyright 2003 Harvard Business School Publishing Corporation
All rights reserved
Printed in the United States of America

07 06 05 04 03   5 4 3 2 1

Library of Congress Cataloging-in-Publication Data
Harvard business essentials: business communication.
p. cm. — (The Harvard business essentials series)
Includes bibliographical references (p.   ) and index.
ISBN 1-59139-113-X (alk. paper)
1. Business communication.
I. Title: Business communication.
II. Series.
HF5718 .H2917 2003
651.7—dc21
2003005927

Contents

Introduction   ix

1 Good Writing   **1**
It Begins with Principles

    Have a Clear Purpose   2
    Be Audience Focused   3
    State Your Key Message Clearly   6
    Stay on Topic   6
    Observe Economy of Words   8
    Use Simple Sentences   9
    Consider Your Delivery Strategy   11
    Summing Up   14

2 Start–Up Strategies   **17**
Your Launch Point

    Questioning Method   18
    Traditional Outline Method   20
    Brainstorm Outline Method   22
    Free Writing Method   25
    Scoping Your Project   26
    Summing Up   27

3 The First Draft   **29**
Getting It Down

    Get It Down First   30
    Build on Strong Paragraphs   32

Create Transitions 36
Use Design Elements to Lighten the Reader's Load 38
Summing Up 41

4 Getting It Right **43**
The Editing Craft

Editing for Content 44
Editing for Style 47
Tighten and Sharpen Those Sentences 51
Editing for Accuracy 56
Summing Up 59

5 Everyday Writing **61**
Memos, Letters, and E-mail

Writing Effective Memos 62
Business Letters That Do the Job 67
Making the Most of E-mail 72
Summing Up 77

6 Presentations **79**
Timeless Principles

Presentations: The Greek Way 80
Four Rhetorical Devices 85
Three Learning Styles 87
Aim for the Head *and* the Heart 90
Summing Up 93

7 Backstage **95**
Preparing Your Presentation

Step 1: Define Your Objective 96
Step 2: Understand the Audience 97
Step 3: Decide What to Say 98
Step 4: Get Organized 99
Step 5: Develop Effective Visuals 101
Step 6: Rehearse 104
Summing Up 105

8 Show Time **107**

Making an Effective Delivery

Speaking Effectively 108

Projecting a Positive Image 109

Keeping the Audience Engaged 110

Handling Questions 112

Making Group Presentations 116

Dealing with Stage Fright 117

Evaluating Your Presentation 118

Summing Up 119

9 Dialogue **121**

The Ultimate Communication

Understanding the Other Person 123

Seeing Yourself (or Your Company) from the

Other Person's Perspective 124

Creating Dialogue 126

Summing Up 131

Appendix A **133**

Useful Implementation Tools

Appendix B **139**

Writing the Perfect Job Application Cover Letter

Appendix C **143**

Commonsense Rules for Presentation Visuals

Notes **151**

Glossary **153**

For Further Reading **155**

Index **157**

About the Subject Adviser **161**

About the Writer **162**

Introduction

Communication is an essential function of enterprise. Whether written or oral, it is the conduit through which an enterprise speaks to its customers. It is management's mechanism for influencing employees and directing the work they do. And it is the means through which employees provide the information and feedback that management needs to make sound decisions. An organization that is clear, consistent, and effective in its communications with customers, employees, shareholders, creditors, and the community is in a good position to establish trust and to elicit their collaboration.

What is true about communication at the enterprise level applies equally at the individual level. People who are good communicators are more successful at advancing in their careers, other factors being equal. Think for a moment about the people you've most admired in your own professional life—people who have moved ahead to leadership positions. They may be colleagues, division heads, CEOs, managers, board members, or industry spokespersons. In addition to having other qualities, these people are probably very good communicators, right? When they speak to a group, send a letter, or talk to you one-on-one, their messages are thought-out, focused, and purposeful. They use every communication opportunity to engage people, share information, or advance their agendas.

Communication skills are an essential element of leadership. Scholars have known for a long time that effective leaders excel at communicating purpose, ideas, and direction to others. Though few would be described as eloquent, all effective leaders are clear and consistent in their communications—and that inspires confidence in others.

What's Ahead

Business Communication, part of the Harvard Business Essentials series, addresses communication at the individual level. The aim is to help you become a more effective communicator—in your writing, in your presentations, and in your one-on-one dealings with others—and is organized accordingly.

The first five chapters will help you with effective writing. The next three address formal presentations. Chapter 9, the last chapter, discusses what makes one-on-one interactions different from all other forms of communication.

Chapter 1 explains a number of principles that you should keep in mind before you tap out a single word on the computer. These principles are concerned with the purpose of your communication, the audience and its needs, the message you want the audience to walk away with, and the best medium and timing of delivery.

Chapter 2 aims to get you started—one of the toughest parts of written communication. It offers many suggestions for overcoming writer's block.

Chapter 3 explains how to create a reasonably good first draft. This job begins with getting your thoughts out in the open, where they can be logically organized.

Once the draft is created, it will need to be edited for style, content, and accuracy—the subject of chapter 4. Some styles are appropriate for directing action, conveying facts, or delivering news—good and bad. Others are more appropriate for being convincing. You'll learn how to choose a style that matches your purpose and how to fine-tune your writing.

Once you've learned the principles of good writing and how to draft and edit your work, you can apply what you've learned to virtually any form of written document: a report, a letter, and so forth. In chapter 5, we take up the particulars of the three most common written forms: memos, letters, and e-mail. Each has features you need to understand if you want to get your ideas across—and stay out of trouble.

Chapters 6 through 8 involve formal presentations in which you have to stand and deliver in front of a live audience. These chapters explain the principles and practical tools for improving your presentations and for overcoming the fear that many people experience as they stand before an audience.

Chapter 9 is concerned with the one-on-one communication that characterizes the majority of our interpersonal encounters in the workplace. Here you'll learn how to understand the other person's perspective and to deal with the other person's perception of you. You'll also gain insights into the importance of dialogue, the most productive form of communication between people.

You'll find that the vocabulary used in these chapters is generally familiar and straightforward. Nevertheless, the book contains a helpful glossary of key terms, which are italicized when they are first introduced in the text.

Three short appendixes supplement the information provided in the rest of the book. Appendix A offers worksheets and checklists you may find useful when planning an oral presentation or a written document. One special letter form—the job application cover letter—is detailed in appendix B. You'll find a primer on the design and use of presentation visuals at the end of the book, in appendix C. In addition, the Harvard Business Essentials Web site, www. elearning.hbsp.org/businesstools, offers free, interactive versions of the tools introduced in this series.

This book is based on numerous books, articles, and online productions of Harvard Business School Publishing. Particularly useful were articles prepared by staff writers for the *Harvard Management Communication Letter*, and modules on business writing and presentations in Harvard ManageMentor, an online management resource. Some chapters on strategic business writing and writing productivity draw from books written by Deborah Dumaine, founder and president of Better Communications (www.writetothetop.com).

1

Good Writing

It Begins with Principles

Key Topics Covered in This Chapter

- *Having a clear purpose*

- *Being audience focused*

- *Stating your key message clearly*

- *Staying on topic*

- *Observing economy of words*

- *Using simple sentences*

- *Considering your delivery strategy*

EFFECTIVE business writing rests on a foundation of principles developed over the centuries. In this chapter, we explore these principles. Master them, and you'll know how to handle the many different writing tasks that come your way: memos, e-mails, letters, reports, and so forth.

Have a Clear Purpose

Literary writing expresses the writer's feelings. Business writing, on the other hand, is utilitarian, aiming to serve any one of many purposes. Here are just a few purposes of business writing:

- **To explain or justify actions already taken:** "Given that situation, we have determined that the best course of action is to reject all current bids and to seek others."

- **To convey information, as in a research report or the promulgation of a new company policy:** "Management wants all employees to know that the floggings will stop as soon as we have evidence of improved morale."

- **To influence the reader to take some action:** "I hope that you will find that our new, Web-based cash management services can reduce your working capital requirements and save you money."

- **To deliver good or bad news:** "Unfortunately, the engine fire you reported occurred one day after the expiration of the warranty period."

- **To direct action:** "Your team should complete and deliver the product specifications by May 1."

So the first thing you should ask yourself is, "What is my reason for writing this document? What do I aim to accomplish?" Keep that purpose uppermost in your mind as you begin writing, and you will be observing the first principle of business writing. Jot the purpose down at the beginning of your draft as a reminder, and refer back to it as you proceed. Doing so will help you stay on course and assure that your writing serves its stated purpose.

And once you've finished your draft, ask yourself, "Has this document fulfilled my stated purpose?" Many writers, in attending to the mundane tasks of preparing a document, lose track of their purpose for writing. Don't make that mistake.

Be Audience Focused

Just about every businessperson understands the critical importance of being customer focused. The customer is, after all, the source of the economic value sought by the organization—a value that can only be extracted if the customer perceives value in what the organization has to offer. Being customer focused means understanding customer preferences and attitudes, how customers perceive value, how they want to be served, and their hot buttons (i.e., what really gets their attention).

There's a clear analogy between the business principle of customer focus and the writing principle of audience focus. Just as a company won't connect with its customers if it fails to understand them, their needs, and how they prefer to be served, you won't connect with your readers if you don't understand them, their needs, and how they prefer to receive information. Will your readers be receptive, indifferent, or resistant to your message? Do they already know a little or a lot about the subject? How much technical information can these readers digest? What are their styles of processing information, and how can you match these styles? That is, do these readers need visual content, or will words suffice? Since reading your document will require their time and attention, what's in it for them?

Case Study: Applying the Audience-Focus Principle

Herb is the product manager for a line of consumer electronic products. With a new gizmo in the early stages of development, Herb knows that it's now time to bring the R&D, marketing, and manufacturing people together. Their collaboration is the company's best assurance that the new product will (1) meet customer requirements and (2) be designed in such a way that the manufacturing division will be able to build them efficiently.

Herb determines that he should write a memo as the first step in building collaboration between the three different groups. Here are some audience issues Herb should consider before he composes the memo:

- **His relationship with the readers:** Since the readers—personnel in marketing, R&D, and manufacturing—do not work directly for Herb, he has no authority over them. A few actually outrank Herb. Given these facts, Herb cannot command or direct his readers; he must elicit their collaboration through persuasion.

- **Different information processing styles:** Herb knows that the marketing people are highly verbal and intuitive, whereas most of the R&D and manufacturing people are engineers; they are less verbal and respond better to data and analysis. He must craft his message with this knowledge in mind.

- **What they already know:** Each member of Herb's audience is familiar with the new gizmo under development, its technical features, and the target market. Consequently, Herb will not have to explain these aspects. But the broader marketing and manufacturing issues have not been resolved.

- **Divergent interests:** Even though all three groups depend on the effectiveness of the corporation for their well-being, each of the three functions—R&D, marketing, and manufacturing—tends to fixate on its own immediate issues. Thus, Herb must communicate in a way that will satisfy these very different parties.

Here's the memo that he wrote:

July 14, 2002

To: Carl Jones, Emma Smith, Roland Carrero, Justine Roussel, Lynn Ravenscroft

From: Herb Bacon

Subject: Time for Gizmo 5 cross-functional planning

As you know, design specs for the Gizmo 5 electronic garlic press are moving forward within R&D. That means that it's time to begin planning for the new product's marketing and manufacturing. Early cross-function planning helped make the Gizmo 4 a tremendous success, and I know that we are all eager to repeat the experience. Great things happen when we put our heads together to focus on a problem. Agenda items will include (1) user benefits and (2) product specs and manufacturability.

I would like to schedule an initial meeting for noon, Monday, August 5, in our small conference room. Lunch will be provided. Does that work for you?

Herb

Notice how Herb does not command or direct his readers, but tactfully elicits their collaboration by giving a clear reason for the meeting—and for his memo. Note too that he suggests benefits for all the readers—marketing, R&D, and manufacturing.

State Your Key Message Clearly

The key message is what you want readers to remember. In contemporary business-speak, it's the so-called take-away. That message should be clear and compact—just a sentence or two for the typical business communiqué. Most communication experts say that if you cannot get the message down to that length, you probably are not clear about what you want to say. The sooner you can isolate the key message into one or two sentences, the easier it will be to write the entire document.

If you experience difficulty in isolating a clear and compact key message, the reason may be that you're struggling to cover two unrelated messages in the same document. In this case, write two separate documents. Stick to one topic per document, and your writing will have more impact.

In most cases, your key message should be stated at or near the very beginning, with the rest of the piece used to flesh out the details or to provide supporting evidence. Doing so assures that skimmers will pick it up. They may or may not want to probe deeper.

Isolating the key message is especially challenging when a committee is involved. A committee generally has members with different viewpoints, and each person often insists on having his or her view represented in a document, inadvertently weakening the focus.

The case study underscores the challenge of writing on behalf of committees. The best antidote is to educate committee members on the importance of drafting focused documents with single themes. When more than one message needs to be communicated, encourage the committee to use more than one document.

Stay on Topic

Many attribute Bill Clinton's victory over George Herbert Walker Bush in the U.S. presidential election of 1992 to Clinton's strategy of continually hammering his opponent on the weak state of the economy. For Clinton, staying on message didn't come naturally. He was capable of expounding on policy issues from A to Z, and enjoyed doing so. This is why his political strategist, James Carville, was always there to remind him of the catchphrase, "It's the economy, stupid!"

Case Study: Too Many Cooks . . .

Edna was an active volunteer in a nonprofit organization whose goal was to revitalize the downtown of her community. Her team had just completed a detailed survey of downtown shoppers, workers, and visitors, and the organization's board had asked her to draft a press release about its findings. Those findings pointed to substantial dissatisfaction with the quality and variety of the town's retail base, which focused almost exclusively on summer tourists to the exclusion of year-round residents and downtown workers.

Edna drafted a press release and submitted it to the board for approval. Its key message was "The survey has identified a serious mismatch between current retail offerings and the express needs of the downtown population." This message made sense to Edna and to everyone else who had analyzed the survey data. But some board members had other ideas. "I think that it projects a negative image," the director of the Chamber of Commerce complained. "We should also say something about the things that people like about our stores."

"Yes," agreed the director of the organization. "And we need to tell readers about all the things we're doing to make things better—our calendar of outdoor events, our merchandising seminars, and so forth. Otherwise, people will think that we aren't doing anything."

Seeing an opportunity, two other board members chimed in with their ideas. By the end of the meeting, the board had given Edna a list of three topics—in addition to the survey results—that it wanted her to include in the press release. But to include these other topics would mean diluting the strong, clear message that Edna had originally crafted.

Carville sensed that the economy was the issue of greatest concern to voters that year and that Clinton's verbal forays into foreign policy, military spending, school lunch programs, and other issues would dissipate his effectiveness and appeal. Consequently, he urged the candidate to keep hammering away on this important issue.

For a writer, staying on message means maintaining a solid connection to the key message. In practical terms this means steering clear of unrelated or loosely related subjects that just happen to be on your mind. It means not slathering on a pile of data and details that obscure the bottom-line message. Supporting data is often necessary, especially when your goal is to convey information or to convince readers. But supporting data should always be linked to the message.

Observe Economy of Words

If you're like most of us, your high school and college instructors periodically required essays or reports of some minimum length. "Give me an essay on the women's suffrage movement by the end of next week—no less than a thousand words," they would tell you, or something to that effect. Though well meaning, the assignments had an unintended consequence: We learned how to take the four hundred words of solid information we had and combine them with six hundred words of blather to reach the assigned word count. Consider this example:

> *The mass movement for women's suffrage in the United States of America—that is, the campaign to give U.S. citizens of the female gender the right to go to the polls and vote for the candidates of their choice in any given election like everybody else—was of monumental importance in the history of the United States of America. It was stupendous in its consequences and scope, involved thousands upon thousands of people—women, men, and others—and its outcome affects how we live, work, and participate in the political process to this very day.*

Sentences like these would advance a student 8 percent of the way toward the thousand-word goal without their saying anything in particular.

In the business world, there are no minimum lengths for written communiqués. In fact, shorter is always better if it communicates the required information. Business writers are advised to heed rule 17 in Strunk and White's timeless *The Elements of Style*, which advises the writer to omit needless words: "Vigorous writing is concise. A sentence should contain no unnecessary words, a paragraph no unnecessary sentences, for the same reason that a drawing should have no unnecessary lines and a machine no unnecessary parts. This requires not that the writer make all his sentences short, or that he avoid all detail and treat his subjects only in outline, but that every word tell."[1]

This quote from Strunk and White is itself a perfect model of their rule. They use no unnecessary words; every word makes a contribution.

Economy of words has two big benefits: Your key message stands out, and it saves your readers valuable time.

Use Simple Sentences

The sentence is the basic unit of written expression. Most sentences make a statement. The statement can be simple or complex:

- *Joan wrote.*

- *Joan wrote a letter.*

- *Joan wrote an apologetic letter.*

- *At her boss's suggestion, Joan wrote an apologetic letter.*

- *At her boss's suggestion, Joan wrote an apologetic letter to the disgruntled customers.*

- *At her boss's suggestion, Joan wrote an apologetic letter to the five disgruntled customers who threatened to sue.*

- *At her boss's suggestion, and with the help of corporate counsel, Joan wrote an apologetic letter to the five disgruntled customers who threatened to sue.*

- *At her boss's suggestion, and with the help of corporate counsel, Joan wrote an apologetic letter to the five disgruntled customers who threatened to sue; each was urged to return his purchase for a full refund.*

This process of sentence "complexification" could go on and on. Sentences are made more complex (and impart more information) as we add objects ("a letter"), clauses ("At her boss's urging"), adjectives ("disgruntled"), and create compound sentences ("each was urged ..."). Packing more information into each sentence is not necessarily bad. Nor does it violate rules of grammar if done properly. However, complexity contains two potential problems. First, complex sentences make the reader work harder. Second, complexity may confuse.

As a writer, your challenge is to know when a sentence has reached its optimal carrying capacity. Here, knowledge of the audience is a useful guide. In the preceding example sentences, do the readers need to know that Joan's boss suggested the letter? Or that corporate counsel was brought in? Is the fact that there were five disgruntled customers relevant? If these bits of information are not necessary, consider eliminating them. If they are necessary, you may use any of the sentences in their current states of complexity or, to make the message easier to swallow, break it into several, less complex sentences.

Both literary writing and business writing in the United States have undergone a gradual evolution from complex to simpler sentences. Consider the two following examples. The first is from Nathaniel Hawthorne's *The House of the Seven Gables*, published in the 1850s; the second is the last line in Ernest Hemingway's 1940 work, *For Whom the Bell Tolls*.

The aspect of the venerable mansion has always affected me like a human countenance, bearing the traces not merely of outward storm and sunshine, but expressive also of the long lapse of mortal life, and accompanying vicissitudes, that have passed within.[2]

He could feel his heart beating against the pine needle floor of the forest.[3]

Hawthorne's sentence is long, complex in structure, and elegant in word usage. Hemingway's, in contrast, is simple and spare—no doubt the product of his early newspaper career. A sharp-penciled newsroom editor probably taught young Hemingway to drop the flowery phrases and three-line sentences and to concentrate on putting his information into tight, little packages. You should follow Hemingway's lead with your business writing.

Consider Your Delivery Strategy

Our final principle concerns authorship, timing, and format. Your message will have more impact if it comes from the right person, at the right time, and in the right format.

Authorship

Before you begin writing, consider *from whom* the communication should come. Should it come from you? Your boss? The entire team? The choice is bound to make a difference in reader impact.

Consider the Declaration of Independence. Thomas Jefferson is credited with drafting the declaration that formally separated the North American colonies from Great Britain. But the paper included the signatures of representatives from each of the colonies. A document written and signed by Jefferson alone would have been well received in his native Virginia, but poorly received elsewhere. Those added signatures indicated agreement among the colony's leaders and assured that the document would have widespread credibility.

Timing

Make sure that you are not writing your document too early or too late. If you write too early, people won't be ready to focus on the issue you're raising. If you wait too long, you'll lose the opportunity to influence the outcome.

Consider the case of Lloyd, a management consultant whose forthcoming book, *The Ten Secrets of Customer Service*, was scheduled for publication in September 2002. Eager to create buzz about his book, Lloyd drafted a two-thousand-word article on the ten secrets and submitted it to a popular business magazine. Unfortunately, the magazine published the article in June 2002, four months too early to serve Lloyd's purpose. By the time his book was published, the buzz had faded.

Format

The format of your writing will also affect its impact on readers. Should it be a formal letter, a memo, or an e-mail? And as long as you're considering the format issue, would a verbal presentation of your message be more effective? The best format for a message is determined by issues we've already discussed: the writer's purpose, the intended audience, and the information the writer is trying to convey. Consider the following case.

Case Study: Form Often Is Function

Helen's staff had just finished a research study on how customers perceive the quality of her company's products and customer service. The findings of the study, its methodology, and supporting data were currently collected in a seventy-page binder. Helen was wondering how best to transmit this information. She knew that some people would want to learn all the details of customer perceptions. Others would want to know how she arrived at her findings—that is, they would want to know her methodology. Some would simply want the bottom line of customer perceptions. And still others—number crunchers in the accounts payable department, for example—would not be the least bit interested. She could hand out copies of the binder, but that format would be inappropriate for many people.

Let's consider two of Helen's options. She could send a memo or an e-mail with a summary of her findings, or she could send the same summary by memo or e-mail, but with this postscript: "The complete study, and a description of its methodology, is available. Call extension 456 to obtain a copy."

This second option would seem to solve her problem but, like the first, is a passive option. People could easily ignore Helen's communication. And since it's in written form, it is also a one-way communication. One-way communication is useful for disseminating simple forms of information (e.g., "The cafeteria will be closed at 2 P.M. tomorrow to accommodate the remodeling program"), but complex information generally has higher impact and imparts greater value if presented verbally and surrounded by dialogue. Thus, Helen might consider this three-pronged alternative:

1. Communicate a written summary of findings by memo or e-mail.

2. Invite anyone interested in the methodology or other details to obtain the full seventy-page report.

3. Invite management and other key parties to a stand-up presentation of the study's findings. This presentation and dialogue between the attendees would enhance the impact of Helen's study on the right people and create further dialogue.

Thus, the ideal format for your communications requires plenty of thought. Even if you stick to a written format, you must consider how best to format and distribute it to obtain the greatest impact. And you need to think about supplementing a written format with other approaches.

Summing Up

This chapter has examined the principles on which good writing is based. These principles apply to all forms of written communication: memos, letters, reports, and so forth. And as you can probably see, most of these principles apply to nonwritten communication as well. In a nutshell, the principles are these:

- **Have a clear purpose.** Business writing can serve many purposes. Never begin writing before you've established in your own mind the purpose for which you are communicating and what you hope to accomplish.

- **Be audience focused.** Communication—in any form—won't do its job if it fails to consider the needs, attitudes, and information preferences of the intended audience. Be attuned to these audience characteristics as you write, and your message will have greater impact.

- **State your key message clearly.** Always think about the message you'd like your audience to take away. The message should be clear and compact. For most business writing, this means just a sentence or two.

- **Stay on topic.** Your key message is your main connection to the audience. For any single piece of writing, you are usually better off sticking with your key point and not getting into other issues. Switching to other topics risks a break in the audience connection.

- **Observe economy of words.** Every word should make a contribution. Unnecessary words are like wisps of fog that obscure what you are trying to say. Clear them away, and your key message will stand out.

- **Use simple sentences.** Sentences are your basic units of expression. Keep them short and uncomplicated, and your readers will have an easier time catching your message.

- **Consider your delivery strategy.** Delivery strategy is about authorship, timing, and format. In terms of impact and what you hope to accomplish, are you the right person to be delivering the message, or should it be someone else? Have you chosen the best time to deliver it? And is the written word the best format? Would a phone call or a stand-up presentation be more effective?

Start–Up Strategies

Your Launch Point

Key Topics Covered in This Chapter

- *Questioning method*

- *Traditional outline method*

- *Brainstorm outline method*

- *Free writing method*

- *Scoping your work*

IMPLY GETTING started is one of the hardest parts of writing. It's often hard to know just where to begin. Call it writer's block. Call it a lack of inspiration. Whatever you call it, getting stuck at the beginning of a writing task can leave a writer frustrated and sometimes completely unable to communicate a simple business message.

Some people try to get started by clearing off their desks, checking their e-mail, or making a cup of tea—or all three. They hope that by the time these tasks are finished, a light will have gone on and the way forward will be obvious. But this is wishful thinking. The light won't go on until the writer actively engages in the task.

This chapter offers four methods for getting started.[1] The first we call the *questioning* method. It puts you in your readers' shoes. The second is the *traditional outlining* approach you probably learned in school. The third is a *brainstorming* approach. And if none of these works, there is the *free writing* method, which encourages your imagination to roam freely. One or several of these methods can get your writing off to a good start.

Questioning Method

If you're stuck in neutral, one way to get into gear is to anticipate the questions your readers might have about your topic. What will they want to know about it? For example, Gillian had to write a memo introducing a weekly interdepartmental meeting of collaborators on a new product launch. Trying to anticipate her readers' concerns, she produced the following questions:

- Why are we having these new meetings?

- Must I attend?

- What will be on the agenda?

- What must I prepare for the meetings?

- When will the meetings begin?

By turning those questions into affirmative statements, Gillian can create the list of points she'll want to cover in her memo. She can also use them as organizing points in her memo:

January 11, 2003

To: Oscar Haywood, JoAnn Dempsey, Raul Vegas, Emily Amherst
From: Gillian Greystone
Regarding: XRP-1 launch meetings

Now that the XRP-1 digital camera design has been approved by management, the marketing department is sponsoring a series of meetings in anticipation of the product launch. These meetings will coordinate activities between R&D, manufacturing, customer service, and marketing, with the goal of maximizing the success of the XRP-1. We know from experience with the Q-3 series product launches that coordination between units is our best assurance of that success. Everyone involved with the XRP-1 is expected to participate. COO David Duffy will be there to represent senior management. Through December, meetings will be monthly, with the first scheduled for Tuesday, August 10, 2–4 P.M., in the North Wing conference room. Meeting frequency will increase as we approach the actual launch date.

The focus of the August 10 meeting will be on forming teams around key aspects of the launch process. The agenda is attached. Participants should come prepared to discuss their department's XRP-1 work plans.

Please call me at extension 123 if you have questions.
Gillian

Notice how Gillian's memo answered each of her anticipated questions:

- **Why are we having these new meetings?** (to coordinate the launch, and because experience shows that coordination is the best assurance of launch success)

- **Must I attend?** (yes, if you're involved in the XRP-1 project)

- **What will be on the agenda?** (Gillian has stated the general focus of the agenda in her memo, with the details attached)

- **What must I prepare for the meetings?** (for the first meeting, come prepared with your unit's work plans)

- **When will the meetings begin?** (August 10)

Although the questioning method is very useful in jump-starting your writing, it is only as effective as a person's ability to anticipate questions that the readers are likely to ask. This underscores the importance of understanding the audience—one of the writing principles described in chapter 1. If you are not totally familiar with your audience, enlist someone with that familiarity to augment your list of anticipated questions. For example, Gillian might have called a friend in the R&D department to ask for her anticipated questions.

Traditional Outline Method

You probably learned in school to start writing with a traditional outline. This method receives mixed results: Some writers swear by it; others swear *at* it. The traditional outline seems to work best for those who can picture a logical structure for a document before writing it.

A traditional outline uses letters and roman and arabic numerals to indicate levels of information. Roman numbers identify the highest-level headings, with capital letter headings (A, B, C, and so forth) nested under them. More details may be nested under those capital letter headings in the form of arabic numerals (1, 2, 3, and so forth). The following example shows the initial outlines for chapters 1 and 2 of this book. Notice that the first roman number is "Principles of good writing." There are four capital letter headings beneath this (A, B, C, D), and B and D break out further details.

I. Principles of good writing
    A. Clear purpose
    B. Recognizes the needs and attitudes of the audience
        1. How to determine audience needs and attitudes
        2. A practical example
    C. Contains a "bottom line" message
    D. Is delivered by the right person, at the right time, in the right format
        1. The right person
        2. The timing question
        3. Different formats for different purposes
            a. Letter versus memo
            b. E-mail
            c. Combining written and personal presentations

II. Start-up strategies
    A. Questioning
    B. Outlining
    C. Brainstorming
    D. Free writing
    E. Scoping your project

Theoretically, you can outline your writing using much more fine-grained nesting of subtopics:

I. First-level heading
    A. Second-level heading
        1. Third-level heading
            a. Fourth-level heading

$$(1) \text{ Fifth-level heading}$$
$$(a) \text{ Sixth-level heading}$$
$$\text{i. Seventh-level heading}$$

And so forth. This level of detail in an outline is generally unnecessary. People can usually plan out everything they need to cover within three levels of headings (roman numerals, capital letters, and arabic numerals).

The traditional outline method has many advantages. It is especially useful if you are an inexperienced writer, if you need to cover a complex subject and want to avoid leaving out any important points, or if you want to maximize the logic of your writing.

Once you have an outline in front of you, ask these questions:

- Are all the topics and subtopics I need to cover listed here?

- Are they arranged in a logical sequence?

- Is there a clear beginning, middle, and ending?

If you find yourself saying no to the first question, try adding subheadings to your existing headings. In other words, break out an existing heading into greater detail. If you are unhappy with the second question, try moving things around until you are satisfied with the logic and flow of your organization. Do the same if you cannot see a clear beginning, middle, and end to your piece.

At this point, you can begin writing or use index cards to gather the information you need to flesh out each line of the outline. You'll know where you're going and what you need to complete the piece.

Brainstorm Outline Method

The brainstorm outline is a free-association approach to generating the ideas that will go into your writing. You can use it whether you are the sole author or a member of a writing team. It's particularly useful with groups since, as an "idea dump," the brainstorming method can get everyone's ideas onto the table at the very beginning.

In brainstorm outlining, you jot down ideas as they come into your head. Those thoughts then become the bases for other ideas. If all goes well, you (or your team) will have surfaced all the key ideas surrounding your topic.

Here's a little trick for brainstorm outlining. Draw a circle in the middle of a blank sheet of paper. Write your purpose inside that circle. Your purpose is the reason you're writing the document. The purpose may be to report specific activities, to persuade readers to take some course of action, to describe a situation that needs improvement, or something else.

As ideas related to that purpose come to mind, draw lines from the circle, like the spokes of a wheel, and write each idea on a line. If an idea inspires other related ideas, draw branching lines off from

Case Study: Brainstorming in Action

Jim, a consultant, was working with a nine-person team whose assignment was to develop a vision statement for their city's downtown revitalization project. The committee wasn't sure where to begin. So Jim set up a flip chart and drew a circle in the center. He wrote "Our Vision" within the circle.

"How would we ideally like the downtown to look at the end of our work?" he asked the team. That question inspired ideas from just about everyone.

"It wouldn't be dead after sundown," said one. "People would be sitting in outdoor cafés during nice weather. They'd be shopping and visiting with friends."

"So, more evening activity would be part of the vision?" Jim asked, drawing a line from the circle and labeling it "Evening Activity."

"Exactly."

Several agreed and went a step further. "Attractive downtown lighting would help make that possible," they said. "It would make the area more appealing and improve public

Continued

safety." Jim nodded and drew a line labeled "Better Lighting" from "Evening Activity."

"The downtown won't be dominated by tourist shops that are closed half the year," piped in another. "We'd have retail stores that cater to people who live and work here year-round instead of the schlocky T-shirt shops we have now. As it stands, the downtown stores don't have the things we want."

"Are you saying that the downtown has the wrong retail mix?" Jim asked. All nodded in agreement. "Well, what do you think would be a more suitable mix?" This question drew many responses, such as more apparel stores and a gourmet food store, which Jim duly recorded.

"And if we could get the city, the Art Institute, the Chamber of Commerce, and the Tourist Board to work together, maybe they could create a year-round schedule of events and fairs that would bring more people downtown—especially at night."

The ideas kept coming for another twenty minutes, and Jim recorded them as they surfaced. By then a brainstorm outline had taken shape on the flip chart (figure 2-1). Like a traditional outline, it contained major headings with related headings nested under them. The team used the outline in developing a draft vision statement for the downtown revitalization project. Here is the first paragraph from that statement:

> *The downtown bustles with activity day and night, and year-round. Its well-lighted retail businesses stay open into the night and appeal to both residents and tourists. There are many things to do, from shopping in specialty stores and gourmet shops to congregating at outdoor cafés along the revitalized waterfront. A full slate of downtown events and fairs makes the downtown a magnet to residents and visitors alike.*

the initial line, and write your ideas on them. If you get an idea entirely separate from the ideas you've recorded so far, draw a new line from the center circle. Continue to generate ideas, drawing lines

FIGURE 2-1

Brainstorm Outline Example

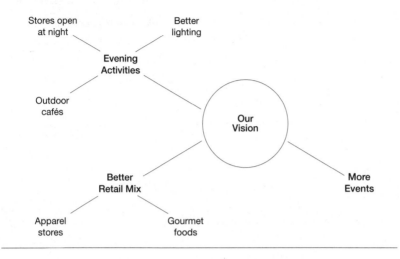

from the center circle and from other lines until new or related ideas no longer appear.

As you can probably tell from this case study, you need to exercise care in defining the main idea categories that pop out of the "purpose" circle. Make them general categories, and you'll be better able to attach related ideas to them. Once you have them organized, those ideas are the topics you'll want to cover in your writing.

Free Writing Method

When you're really stuck with writer's block, also known as blank screen syndrome, free writing is the best solution. Like the brainstorm outline, free writing allows your imagination to roam, thus facilitating the expression of great ideas. The most important rule to remember about free writing is that there are *no* rules.

Put pen to paper or fingers to keyboard, and let your mind wander. Write down anything that comes into your head, even if it has nothing to do with your writing topic. Do this for at least ten minutes to get the ideas flowing. When you get stuck, write that down, too: "I'm stuck! I'm stuck." Don't stop, no matter what. Don't edit your work, either. If you're working at your computer, darkening the screen may help you keep yourself from editing prematurely.

When you've finished free writing, read what you've set down, highlighting important points and ideas. Then organize those points and ideas into logical categories, just as you would in a traditional outline or its brainstorming counterpart. At that point, you're almost ready to begin drafting your document.

Scoping Your Project

We have now offered four methods for getting started. Any of them can help you draw out the ideas you'll use to populate your written document. But before you actually begin tapping the keys, you should scope your project. By *scoping* we mean determining the breadth of your subject and how deeply you will cover it. This is something you should do with any prepared form of communication, written and verbal.

To understand the necessity of scoping, imagine that you're preparing a report on weaknesses in your company's marketing function. You could look at this subject broadly, or you could be very focused, examining one or two areas that have the greatest performance problems. Each approach has its merits and demerits, and the choice must be determined by the situation. The two approaches would consider different issues:

Broad Scope

- How marketing contributes to corporate goals

- Historic development of the company's marketing department

- Marketing's human resources

- Challenges past and present

- Areas of specific performance problems

- Potential solutions

Limited Focus

- Two areas of underperformance: dealer support and promotions

- Suggested remedies

As a writer, you must determine how broad or limited the scope of your piece should be, given the factors discussed earlier: your purpose in writing and your audience. In the case of the marketing report just described, you might take a very broad approach if your purpose is to provide information to top management and to a task force assigned to study the department and potential solutions. That audience would want to know as much as possible about the department. On the other hand, you'd probably use the limited-scope alternative if you were communicating to top management about the task force's actual findings: "Here are the problems we've identified, and here are our recommended solutions."

Do a good job of scoping, and you will save yourself and your audience a lot of unnecessary work. What's more, your writing will have the desired level of reader impact.

Summing Up

Having trouble getting your writing task started? Can't think of where to begin or what to say? This chapter explained four methods for getting started:

- **Questioning:** Practitioners of this method try to anticipate the questions their readers will have about the subject. Those questions are turned into affirmative statements that, in turn, are used to form a list of topics that need to be covered.

- **Traditional outline:** This is the start-up method you probably

learned in school. It features the familiar set of roman numerals followed by capital letter headings followed by arabic
numerals, and so forth. It's particularly good when you need a
tight, logical structure to your topic before you start the actual
writing. The level of detail in the traditional outline can be
low or high.

• **Brainstorm outline:** In brainstorming, participants "dump"
their ideas as they occur. One idea can be used to elicit related
or subsidiary ideas. To get the best results from a brainstorming
session, have a moderator jot down the ideas. Then try to
organize them into logical groupings. Those groups are then
the basis for traditional outlining or for active writing.

• **Free writing:** This is a method without rules. The writer simply allows his or her mind to wander, and writes down whatever comes to mind. Activity is more important than direction
with this method. At some point, the writer stops, highlights
the ideas that pertain to the topic, and organizes them for the
writing task ahead.

Any of these methods, or a combination of them, can help you
break through any start-up block. As emphasized, however, once
you have a set of topics or an outline to flesh out in words, do one
more thing: scope it.

• **Scoping:** is the determination of how broadly or narrowly a
subject will be treated. The scope of a piece of writing
depends on the situation. For this reason, then, it is important
that you scope out your work before you begin in earnest.

3

The First Draft

Getting It Down

Key Topics Covered in This Chapter

- *Getting your ideas down*

- *Building on paragraphs*

- *Creating transitions*

- *Using design elements to lighten the reader's load*

CHAPTER 2 described four strategies for getting your writing project started. Each strategy will produce an organized set of ideas or topics that you'll want to address. Scoping the project, also covered in chapter 2, will place boundaries around those ideas and topics, assuring that the breadth and depth of your writing is appropriate for your audience and for your intended purpose.

This chapter introduces the next step: hammering out a first draft. In doing so, it pays attention to four things in particular:

- The importance of getting it down first, without worrying about the niceties of grammar, punctuation, and word choice

- Paragraphs—your basic building blocks

- The use of transitions to help the flow of ideas

- The use of design elements to aid readers

Get It Down First

The consensus advice of business writing experts on developing a first draft is simple: Get it written; get it right later. It's more important to get that first draft written than to master every detail of grammar, punctuation, style, and word choice! Getting it down in rough form has two important benefits. First, it gets the ball rolling. Second, since the writer has only a small investment in the draft, he or she can discard material or change its order rather painlessly.

But where should you begin? Some experts advise beginning where you feel most comfortable. We qualify this suggestion a bit. Assuming that you're using a word processor, try this: Cut and paste your outline (see chapter 2) into a blank page on your screen. Just for fun, let's use the outline we used in writing this chapter as an example:

I. Introduction
II. Getting it down
    A. Benefits
    B. How to begin
III. Pay attention to structure
    A. Beginning
    B. Middle
    C. Ending
IV. Build on strong paragraphs
V. Use design elements to lighten the reader's load
    A. Use headings and subheadings
    B. Break up long blocks of text
    C. Let graphics tell part of the story

Now, once you have the outline on your page, pick one of the major sections and start filling it, just as we have loaded our thoughts about "getting it down" into this section of the chapter. Not sure which section to start with? Don't let indecision hold you back. Go after whichever section seems most comfortable. And don't worry about starting at the very beginning. Most experienced writers save the introductory section until the very end, for two reasons. First, the introduction is often the most difficult and important part. Second, a writer has a much better sense of the piece after having completed the first draft.

Build on Strong Paragraphs

The paragraph is to writing what supporting beams and stringers are to a building.[1] Paragraphs are the essential building blocks of the text. They introduce topics in a larger composition and signal readers that another step in the argument has begun. As such, paragraphs exist primarily for the convenience of the reader, but they also help the writer keep his or her thinking clear and concise as the piece develops. We offer five tips on developing paragraphs.

Begin with What's Familiar, and End with What's New

Just as a good politician begins talking to us about what we already know or have in common, good paragraphs should do the same. Save the new idea for the end. This simple device works because it respects the way the mind builds on what it already knows. Compare the following versions of the same idea. Which is easier to grasp?

> **Version 1:** *The question is whether investors will learn from the shocking free fall in valuation of hitherto high-flying stocks. The recent collapse of Internet stock prices exceeded all the other drops in the stock market in this century.*

> **Version 2:** *Of all the stock market drops in this century, the recent collapse of Internet stock prices was the worst. Will this shocking free fall in valuation teach investors a lesson about high-flying stocks?*

The first version puts the new first and the familiar last, both in the sentences themselves and in the brief paragraph as a whole. The first sentence begins with the question raised by the content of the second half of the sentence. That's confusing. It would be better to write it the other way around, with the idea of the drop in prices followed by the question that the drop raises. Similarly, the second sentence puts the new before the familiar (the recent crash before the older crashes).

The second version gets it right. The paragraph proceeds from the familiar to the new. Then, it repeats the now familiar in order to ask the question that is the point of the paragraph. Note how much clearer and more forceful the second version seems, simply because it obeys this rule of putting the familiar before the new.

Limit the Number of Subjects in Each Paragraph

Most paragraphs are more complicated than the brief example just given, which was deliberately simplified to make a point. Typically, a paragraph will have anywhere from three to a dozen sentences. Each of these sentences will have a subject. The second tip on good paragraph construction is to keep the number of subjects to a minimum without making your writing sound condescending.

Make the Audience the Subject of Key Sentences

Take a look at the opening of one of the best-known speeches of the twentieth century, President John F. Kennedy's inaugural address. Many cite the closing lines ("Ask not what your country can do for you; ask what you can do for your country") as evidence of why the speech struck a chord of patriotism and renewal for a generation of Americans. But Kennedy's speech is more than a collection of a few famous lines. It is a tightly constructed masterpiece of writing that makes what Kennedy has to say personal through its choice of sentence subjects.

> We observe today not a victory of a party but a celebration of freedom—symbolizing an end as well as a beginning—signifying renewal as well as change. For I have sworn before you and Almighty God the same solemn oath our forebears prescribed nearly a century and three-quarters ago.
>
> The world is very different now. For man holds in his mortal hands the power to abolish all forms of human poverty and all forms of human life. And yet the same revolutionary beliefs for which our forebears fought are still at issue around the globe. . . .
>
> We dare not forget today that we are the heirs of that first revolution. Let the word go forth from this time and place, to friend and foe

alike, that the torch has been passed to a new generation of
Americans. . . .

Let every nation know, whether it wishes us well or ill, that we
shall pay any price, bear any burden, meet any hardship, support any
friend, oppose any foe to assure the survival and the success of liberty.
This much we pledge—and more.

The string of subjects in these long, complex opening sentences is tightly controlled and surprisingly simple: We. The world. We. You. What was Kennedy doing? Even while making the overall sentences complex, Kennedy kept the focus on the subjects using the most personal of pronouns: I, we, you, us. The result is that the reader or listener had a sense that Kennedy was speaking personally to him or her, and speaking from the heart. There was no feeling of bureaucratic obfuscation, despite the elaborate sentences and occasionally high-flown prose.

The control of subjects throughout your paragraphs is the second key to giving your reader a sense of coherence and simplicity. You can maintain this control, even when the subject is complicated and the sentences are long.

Does your writing have Kennedy's control? Try this simple test. Take a piece of your own writing. Underline all the subjects of the sentences. If there are more than three or four different subjects in the typical paragraph of average length, then your writing will suffer from incoherence. But use this device with care. If you make all the subjects of your sentences within paragraphs the same, your writing will begin to sound too simple.

Include an Issue, a Point, and a Discussion

Each paragraph should have three elements: an issue, a point, and an appropriate discussion. The issue comes first. It is a statement—in one or more sentences—of what the paragraph is generally about. Next comes the point, a one-sentence statement of the take-away, or your main comment on the issue. Finally, add several sentences of discussion, further amplifying or defending your point with supporting evidence and the like. For example:

> **Issue:** *Employee turnover has become a larger problem this year, both for the industry and for us as a company. Our calculations indicate that turnover cost us roughly $2.3 million last year—up 20 percent from the previous year.*

> **Point:** *This is a cost we can ill afford—and one that we can drastically reduce if we identify the causes of turnover and address them effectively.*

> **Discussion:** *I've asked human-resources director Sandy Milligan to form a task force to address the turnover problem. Employees from each operating unit and key staff areas will join her in that effort. Together they will seek the root causes of turnover and look outside the company for best practices for dealing with it. They will report their findings to management by the end of the third quarter.*

You can vary this structure by putting the point sentence at the very end of the paragraph. But since most readers unconsciously expect to find the point after the issue, you should vary the basic paragraph structure only for a good reason.

Alternatively, Begin with a General Statement

The issue-point-discussion format is not the only approach to effective paragraph construction. Another approach is to begin each paragraph with a general statement, and then explain or elaborate on that statement in subsequent sentences of the paragraph. Here's an example, with the general statement in bold:

> **The bonus plan adopted by the board of directors last week reflects the input of a broad cross section of the corporation.** *First, a task force representing Human Resources, senior management, the board, and Globetrot Consulting LLP sketched out three alternative plans. Those plans were then submitted to the controller, the heads of the operating units, and several middle managers for comment. Their comments and suggestions were incorporated into the final plan.*

The opening statement communicates the idea the writer wants most to get across. The next three sentences provide the underlying specifics that support and flesh out the general statement.

Create Transitions

One of the toughest problems that many writers experience is creating effective transitions between sentences within paragraphs and between paragraphs themselves. Without transitions, readers have trouble seeing the linkage between ideas, and the development of an argument. The writing itself appears choppy and amateurish. Consider this example:

> *Proponents of expanding restaurant seating have failed to provide any estimates of construction, operating costs, and taxes. Without those estimates, any attempt to evaluate their proposal will be a waste of time.*
>
> *No one knows how a doubling of seating will affect annual revenues. Is it reasonable to assume that revenues will double, or is a 75 percent increase a more likely figure?*

This example includes two very different issues: the cost of expanding an existing restaurant, and how revenues might grow if such expansion were made. As stated, we can see no connection between these two issues. Readers would likely ask, "Where are we going with this?" The writer could cure the problem with a transition statement. Let's look at the same sentences, but with a transition (in bold).

> *Proponents of expanding restaurant seating have failed to provide any estimates of construction, operating costs, and taxes. Without those estimates, any attempt to evaluate their proposal will be a waste of time.*
>
> ***Even if construction costs were reasonable and manageable for the operation, we would still be facing a high level of revenue uncertainty.*** *No one knows how a doubling of seating will*

affect annual revenues. Is it reasonable to assume that revenues will double, or is a 75 percent increase a more likely figure?

The transition sentence in this example gives readers a smooth path between the construction costs and the revenue issues.

In many cases, an entire transition sentence is unnecessary. Particular words or phrases can accomplish the same task. Here are some transition words you can use:

consequently	likewise
as a result	meanwhile
in addition	for example
nevertheless	finally
on the other hand	furthermore
until that time	

Note the transition words in the following examples:

*Our inventory managers have kept a tight lid on stocks of finished goods. **Consequently**, working capital requirements have dropped by 8 percent.*

*Many factors cloud the golf course's future revenue stream with uncertainty. **For example**, competition from the new course in Lakeville, the ongoing recession, and the availability of many other forms of recreation in this area threaten the steady patronage that the older course has enjoyed.*

*Yes, we have the funds needed for restaurant expansion. **On the other hand**, we have many other opportunities for applying those funds.*

Now go back and read each of those statements without the connection words. You'll find them choppy and somewhat incoherent. In the first example, the link between tight inventories and reduced working capital requirements would not be explicit. By using the term *consequently*, the writer identifies a causal relationship between the two.

Use Design Elements to Lighten the Reader's Load

Most businesspeople are busy—managers in particular. Your writing must take this into account. Many years ago, Henry Mintzberg published a classic study on how managers spend their time. He characterized the typical manager's day as little more than a series of meetings, unscheduled phone calls, interruptions, and minor crises. Thus, it's not surprising that managers rarely have the time to read everything that crosses their desks. The executive summary placed in the front of many reports is a response to this problem.

Most readers, however, want more than the big picture provided in the executive summary. Given their time constraints, they learn to skim written material; they only drill down to the details when they spot something particularly relevant.

You can facilitate skimming by using *design elements* in your writing. By design elements we mean headings, subheadings, short blocks of text, and graphics. Even white space can be used as a design element.

Design elements are particularly useful in long documents. Used judiciously, they can

- make your written documents more inviting to the reader,

- improve reader comprehension,

- help speed the reader through your material.

Use Headings and Subheadings

Headings and subheadings signal that a new or related topic is about to begin. Both of these characteristics give your work greater eye appeal and "skimmability." You can also use headings and subheadings to impart key ideas. If you look back over the pages of this chapter, you'll see how we've used headings for that purpose. A time-constrained reader could gather the key ideas of the chapter by simply reading these headings and subheadings.

If you use headings and subheadings, be sure that they are nested properly. Doing so will help the reader see the relationship between topics. For example, the subheadings nested under the earlier main heading "Build on Strong Paragraphs" provide specific tips for how to build a strong paragraph. You can differentiate headings and subheadings for your readers as we have throughout this book: through the use of different fonts, capitalization, and indentation.

Break Up Long Blocks of Text

Long, uninterrupted blocks of text are off-putting to readers and are difficult to skim. Headings and subheadings can help you break them into small, identifiable bites. So can short paragraphs. Writing expert Mary Munter recommends that paragraphs average not more than two hundred words, five sentences, or 1½ inches of single-spaced typing.[2]

Numbered lists are another effective way to break up long, intimidating blocks of text and to increase the impact on readers. You can also use them either to summarize key points or to get your ideas across very quickly, as in the following example:

Our study of the restaurant expansion proposal uncovered three negative factors:

1. *The profits of the current operation are substantially overstated because of cost account errors.*

2. *The construction costs estimates put forward by the proponents of the proposal are based on a 1998 bid and do not reflect current costs.*

3. *The assumptions on which future revenues projections are based are, in our view, unreasonably optimistic.*

Notice how the numbered list breaks up the page and gets the writer's conclusions across in a way that they cannot be missed.

Bullets can serve the same purposes as numbered lists. Writers sometimes use bullets as the best way to get information across clearly and succinctly—if not elegantly. You can use bullets for several purposes:

- To highlight a sequence of actions

- To organize a list of items

- To list parts of a whole

Bullets (or numbers) are not needed when you have only one or two elements in your list. In these cases, you can usually manage by saying something like this: "Customers identified two problems with our new coffee blend: It tastes like sludge, and it causes gastric distress."

Let Graphics Tell Part of the Story

When it comes to transmitting lots of numerical data, bar charts and pie charts are hard to beat. Readers can see at a glance what they would otherwise have to extract from many tedious lines of verbiage and numbers. Which of the following would you rather read? Which would make a more memorable impression?

FIGURE 3-1

How People Reach the Downtown

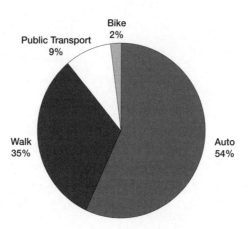

Text only: *Our survey found that 2 percent of the people who come downtown in a typical day do so by bicycle. Nine percent arrive by public transportation. Thirty-five percent respond that they walk to the downtown, whereas the largest single group— 54 percent—arrive by automobile.*

Text and graphics: *According to our survey, people arrive downtown by various means, mostly by automobile (figure 3-1).*

Notice that telling the story with a graphic won't necessarily save you space, but it will give your audience a break from reading text. A graphic generally has more impact than straight text. In the later chapters on presentations, we'll have more on the use of graphics.

One Caution

Don't get carried away with design elements. The modern word processor provides writers with an arsenal of design features: boldface, italics, dozens of font sizes and styles, clip art, chart-making tools, and so forth. Used judiciously, these add to the appearance and readability of your text. Overuse them, however, and you will create the opposite effect and make your work appear amateurish.

There is no general rule about the appropriateness of design features. Every piece is different. When in doubt, use a professionally done piece of a similar nature (e.g., a report or journal article) as a model.

Summing Up

This chapter has explained how to create good first draft material. It emphasized the benefits of getting a good draft completed before you worry about the niceties of grammar, word choice, and punctuation—all of which can be addressed later. We offered one strategy for writers using word processors: cutting and pasting the outline into a blank page, and then developing whichever section of the outline seems easiest.

The bulk of the chapter focused on three tools that writers should consider as they develop the first draft:

- **Building on paragraphs:** Paragraphs are the essential building blocks of written prose. Five tips were offered with respect to paragraphs.

- **Creating transitions:** Transitions help readers move from idea to idea. The text offered suggestions for using either sentences or particular transition words for this purpose.

- **Using design elements to lighten the reader's load:** Design elements such as headings and subheadings, boldface fonts, bulleted and numbered lists, white space, and graphics are effective in helping busy readers process written material. But avoid the temptation to overuse these elements.

Getting It Right

The Editing Craft

Key Topics Covered in This Chapter

- *Editing for content*

- *Editing for style*

- *Tightening and sharpening sentences*

- *Editing for accuracy*

GETTING THAT first draft down is a major hurdle and in many ways the biggest challenge to business writers. The goal is to make sure that all key ideas and supporting arguments are set forth in a logical manner—and in a reader-friendly format. In some respects drafting is as much about logic as about writing.

The next and final steps involve editing—for content, style, clarity, and accuracy. These steps improve the rough-hewn draft and put an attractive polish on it. They make both the finished product and the writer look good!

Editing for Content

After finishing your first draft, you should edit for content, which involves fine-tuning the structure, logic, and message of your document. The surest approach to content editing is to step back and check to see that your piece has an attention-stopping beginning, a well-crafted middle, and an ending that drives your key point or points home.

Check the Beginning

In the writing business, few things are as important as a strong beginning. A strong beginning captures the interest of readers and moves them toward the main points of the piece. Does your beginning give people a reason to continue reading?

One way to capture reader attention comes right out of Sales 101: Indicate the benefits of reading your piece. Consider this example:

Many in our company have been puzzled and frustrated by high turnover among our customers. In some regions, annual turnover exceeds 73 percent. This report identifies the root causes of customer turnover and proposes a number of practical solutions.

In sales parlance, this type of opening provides the "sizzle" that makes people eager to learn more. But good salesmanship describes features as well as benefits, so consider adding key features to your opening prose:

Many in our company have been puzzled and frustrated by high turnover among our customers. In some regions, annual turnover exceeds 73 percent. This report identifies the root causes of customer turnover and proposes several practical solutions, specifically:

- *Revamping the customer call center*

- *A team approach to selling and service*

- *A new method for identifying and targeting high-value customers*

The reader now has a clear idea of the content of the piece and will be attracted to read it, knowing that it identifies problem causes *and* offers very specific solutions.

Look For Compelling Logic in the Middle

Having attracted your readers, you must move beyond the sizzle to the steak. Here, check to see that the paragraphs in the middle of your piece unfold in a progressive and compellingly logical way. Each should add value: to convince, to encourage action, or to simply transmit information. Any paragraph or sentence that fails to add value should be either strengthened or eliminated.

After a first pass through the middle of your piece, double-check to make sure that you've done all that you promised in the opening. For instance, if you were the author of the preceding example, you could ask yourself two questions: "Have I identified the root causes of customer turnover, and have I described three practical solutions as promised?" If the middle section does not deliver on all that was promised, make the necessary adjustments.

Give It a Tight Wrap-Up

Like the beginning, the ending of a written piece is one of the toughest chores. By the time they've said their piece, writers are usually tired of what they're doing and want to quit. "I don't have anything more to say about this," is a typical remark. But a written piece without an ending is incomplete. An ending is needed to close the piece and ease readers out of it. Good endings accomplish one or more things:

Tips for a Good Ending

The following suggestions will help you create a strong ending for any piece of writing:

- **Never introduce new subject matter.** When actors return to the stage for a curtain call, they don't begin a new scene. They bow and make an exit. Likewise, the ending is not a place to introduce new ideas, examples, anecdotes, or other subject matter.

- **Use your own words.** Citing and quoting others in the body of a piece is often appropriate and can be very useful in supporting your statements. The ending, however, is reserved for you. Readers expect the final words to be the author's.

- **Be brief.** The ending should represent a very small part of the total word count. To do otherwise, you would have to violate one or both of the two preceding points.

- Create a sense of closure for the readers

- Reinforce the main points made in the text without rehashing their details

- Alert the readers to action steps for the future

- Urge some type of action on the part of the reader

- Create a satisfying symmetry that brings the readers back to the themes cited in the beginning

Finish off your piece with a strong ending, and you're more likely to satisfy your readers and achieve your goal as a writer.

Editing for Style

"He has an engaging style." "I like her user-friendly style." "Most people are put off by his writing style." Much is made of a writer's style, though almost no one explains what he or she means by it. Fortunately, John Fielden provides a workable definition of style for the business writer: "that choice of words, sentences, and paragraph format which by virtue of being appropriate to the situation and to the power positions of both writer and reader produces the desired reaction and result."[1] As you edit your work, you should try to adopt an appropriate style. But what is an appropriate style? Style, according to Fielden, may be forceful, passive, personal, impersonal, colorful, or colorless. The appropriate choice is determined by the circumstances.

Forceful Style

If you are in a superior position to your readers, or if you seek to compel action, consider using a forceful style. A forceful style makes regular use of the active voice and is very direct. Here are examples of each:

Passive: *A letter should be sent to the customer.*

Active: *Send the customer a letter.*

Indirect: *Unfortunately, management cannot honor your request for a leave of absence at this time.*

Direct: *Your request for a leave of absence is denied.*

Notice in these examples the bureaucratic, unassertive tone of the passive voice and indirect style. The tone of the active voice and direct style, in contrast, is more authoritative and commanding. Think about the situations in which one style or the other would be the most appropriate.

Passive Style

A passive style never goes for the jugular, and it never gives direct orders. It makes its point through suggestion. This may be perfectly appropriate in certain circumstances. So, instead of writing, "Don't waste our time at the next meeting; come prepared," the passive writer would write, "Greater preparation will make the time we spend in meetings more effective." Fielden recommends this style when a person is faced with a negative situation and is writing as a subordinate to some higher authority.

Personal Style

The personal style is conversational and refers often to the writer and reader by name or through personal pronouns (e.g., *I, you, we*): "I like your suggestion for providing GPS systems in the delivery trucks, Jack. Let me know what it would cost to try it on a pilot basis." It also makes heavy use of the active voice. For example, "Please bounce that same idea off Ralph and Harriet. I want to know where they stand on the matter." A personal style is useful when the goal is to deliver good news, to congratulate, or simply to communicate with a peer, a subordinate, or another person with whom you enjoy a congenial relationship.

Impersonal Style

An impersonal style is appropriate when you're delivering bad news, writing a technical report, or simply conveying information to a mixed group of readers (subordinates, peers, and higher-ups). The impersonal style avoids the use of individual names and personal pronouns such as *me, I, we,* and *you.* The author, in fact, disappears behind the text. Thus, impersonal writing lacks the conversational tone of the personal style.

Instead of saying, "We cannot make a decision based on the information that Bill Jones's sales group has submitted," the impersonal stylist would write something quite different: "The information submitted by the Western Sales Group is helpful but insufficient for decision making at the corporate level." This may sound formal and bureaucratic, but it's the appropriate style for the circumstances just described.

Colorful Style

Colorful writing is often appropriate when communicating with nonadversarial readers when the goal is to deliver good news, to congratulate, or to motivate. Superlatives and metaphors are often effective.

To Bob, Sue, Alice, and Al—the "Dream Team" of Acme Sales:

Congratulations on your year-to-date sales figures. I am happy to report that your team has already exceeded its annual goal by $234,000. That puts you "in the money" in terms of the bonus plan and far ahead of all other Acme sales teams. And there are still two months remaining in the fiscal year! I hope that you will use that time to run up the scoreboard still further. Remember that every $1,000 of sales revenue you generate beyond the current total will earn $100 in bonus money for your team. So go for it!

A colorful and exuberant message like this is fitting for its situation, but would be highly inappropriate in many others, for example:

Dear Cissy:

Your husband, Ralph, is really one of a kind and one heck of a bank employee. And I mean really*. What a guy! First he refused to lie facedown on the floor like everyone else in the bank lobby. And then*

*he tried to get the armed robbers to apply for home equity loans!
People around here will be talking about it for years to come.*

*We hope that Ralph's recovery is swift and that he will return to
duty very soon.*

Colorless Style

Some situations, like the case of the bank employee, call for dis-
tinctly *un*colorful writing, in which personal pronouns, adjectives,
active voice, and exuberance are limited.

Fielden notes that there is no right style for every occasion and
purpose: "In business writing, style cannot be considered apart from
the given situation or from the person to whom the writing is
directed."[2] Thus, style and situation—and the goal of your writing—
should be closely linked. You know, for instance, that the style of a
letter written to a friendly colleague must be much different from
the style of one written to an irate customer who has threatened to
sue you. Consider these examples:

Dear Helen:

*It was great seeing you at the national sales meeting last week. Give my
best wishes to Freddie and the rest of the east coast regional sales team.*

Bill

Dear Mr. Raptor:

*We are sorry about the problems you have experienced with our
equipment and regret to hear that you feel that litigation is the best
remedy. Naturally, we would prefer to work with you in finding the
source of the problem and resolving it to your satisfaction. To that end,
I have forwarded your letter to our engineering and customer service
groups. They will be contacting you this week.*

Respectfully,

*William D. Turner
Vice President, North American Sales Group*

In the end, the style of your communication must be dictated by how you perceive the situation, your relationship with the reader, and the goal you hope to accomplish. Here are some of these various factors:

Situation: adversarial, collaborative, negotiating, sales, social, good news, or bad news

Relationship with reader: arms-length, collegial, customer-oriented, impersonal, subordinate, or superior

Goal: to cajole, conciliate, congratulate, convince, greet, inform, persuade, report, or warn

Tighten and Sharpen Those Sentences

Once you've adopted a suitable style for the content of your piece, look closely at the sentences you've used and at the words from which they are constructed. Pay particular attention to each of the following: economy of words, word choices, sentence structure, sentence length, and voice.

Economy of Words

Economy of words was cited in chapter 1 as a principle of good writing. Put that principle to work as you edit your letter, e-mail, report, or other form of communication. Look for opportunities in every sentence to eliminate words that add little or no value. Likewise, if a sentence does nothing to support your message or move your argument forward, cut the entire sentence. Saying the same thing in fewer words and fewer sentences will help keep the attention of readers and add impact to your prose.

Here are typical examples of wordy sentences and how they can be tightened:

Wordy: *I think that we should raise our prices across the board. ("I think" is understood. If you didn't think so, why would you say it?)*

Improved: *We should raise prices across the board.*

Wordy: *Clearly, it's time to change the bonus plan. [Or worse]: It's clear to me that it's time to change the bonus plan. [Clearly is a weasel word used by writers and lawyers who secretly doubt that the situation is clear.]*

Improved: *It's time to change the bonus plan.*

Wordy: *We plan to give consideration to your proposal the next time that the board meets.*

Improved: *We will consider your proposal at the next board meeting.*

Wordy: *What has this department contributed to our goals and objectives?*

Improved: *What has this department contributed to our goals? [Goals and objectives are repeatedly chained together by business-people, even though the words mean the same thing.]*

Finally, here's a sentence that suffers badly from "business BS." If you read it in a memo, you'd probably gag. How would you cut it down to size?

We plan to devote considerable effort to the study of developing requirements and will seek to develop proposed solutions to the various possible needs we can foresee well in advance of the time that a decision will be needed.

The sentence violates every criterion of good business writing. "We plan to" should be "We're acting now." Repeated words, such as *develop* and *developing*, or repeated meanings, such as *considerable* and *well*, are nothing more than padding. Useless modifiers such as *proposed* and *possible* weaken the impact of key nouns. "Will be needed," a passive construction, begs the questions By whom, and when? It's impossible to know what the writer hopes to communicate.

Even accomplished business writers find opportunities to reduce verbiage from their drafts. So, apply a sharp pencil to what you've written. Doing so will make your piece more readable and make its message stand out.

Use Jargon and Bureaucratic Language with Caution

While you're trimming away at unnecessary words, take a look at the kinds of words you're using. Are they straightforward and businesslike, or do they make you sound like a lawyer or government bureaucrat? Are your words part of the readers' vocabulary, or are they the jargon of a small group? More important, are they *appropriate*?

Jargon is not bad and may even be appropriate *if* the reading audience is familiar with the words and their meaning. Consider this statement:

> *The consensus 2003 EPS estimate for DataQuack is $0.34. At the current share price, this would push the company's P/E ratio to around 52, a historic high for the company and a red flag for investors. From a technical viewpoint, however, the ninety-day moving average relative to the S&P 500 trend line is unfavorable.*

Though chock-full of jargon, the preceding statement wouldn't faze an audience of financial analysts and investment managers. They would understand and appreciate the use of these terms. Members of the American Association of Humanities Majors, on the other hand, would probably be mystified.

Consequently, with your audience in mind, aim for simplicity in your word selection. As a rule of thumb, use the simplest words that will communicate your message.

Instead of . . .	Write . . .
remuneration	payment
pending assessment of	until
in consequence of	as a result
henceforth and hereafter	starting today
prioritize	rank
optimal	best

Sentence Structure

Make sure that each sentence has a simple, logical structure and a clearly defined subject, verb, and object. For example, "*Team members* [subject] *will meet* [verb] their QRS Corporation *counterparts* [object] at 2 P.M." Some business writing is so muddy that readers cannot identify the subject or what action is being taken or requested. Very often, the best way to avoid this result is to simplify and make the sentences as direct as possible.

Notice in the following sentences how attention to sentence structure and verbiage can make prose shorter, more direct, and clearer.

It is imperative that our current cost overruns be addressed by the responsible parties, namely, the project managers. [18 words].	*Project managers should explain the reasons for cost overruns. [9 words].*
It's likely that the odor of paint fumes will be perceivable throughout the building, even though control measures will be in place to minimize them. [25 words].	*You may notice paint fumes in the building, but we will do our best to minimize the odor. [18 words.]*
Insofar as the submission of time cards is concerned, it is of the essence that all employees be punctual. [19 words].	*Please submit your time cards on time. [7 words].*

In each of these examples, shorter, more direct sentences make the subject and the requested action stand out.

Sentence Length

Many writing experts say that sentences in business writing should average twelve words. Note the word *average*. You will be more successful in maintaining reader attention if you mix it up. A short sentence every now and then will make your writing more lively. Like this one. On the other hand, a long sentence that flows smoothly from one line to another will change the rhythm of the piece. If you put short and long sentences together effectively, then you'll create reader-pleasing variety.

Voice

Voice indicates the relationship between a sentence's subject and its verb. We addressed active and passive voice earlier in our discussion of appropriate style. Now we will look at how voice relates to sentence structure.

When the subject acts, the sentence has an active voice. When the subject is acted upon, the sentence is in the passive voice:

Active: *The editorial director declared the book out of print.*

Passive: *The book was declared out of print by the editorial director.*

A change in voice does not alter the meaning of a sentence, but it does shift its emphasis. In the first example, the emphasis is on the actor—the editorial director. This puts the sentence in the active voice and makes the editorial director the center of interest. In the second example, the book—and *not* the key actor—is the center of interest; this makes it a passive sentence.

Passive sentences are not always bad or inappropriate. They are useful when the identity of the actor is not your main concern or when you'd like to conceal that identity. For example, you could write, "The book was declared out of print" if you want to play down that it was the editorial director's decision. The classic case of concealment is "Mistakes were made." Countless generations of bureaucrats have used this passive expression to hide the fact that they really screwed up.

Passive sentences are generally appropriate in impersonal reports and technical writing. However, they have several drawbacks. First, passive sentences generally require more words—namely, a helping verb and an extra preposition:

Passive: *Price changes are disliked by customers. [6 words]*

Active: *Customers dislike price changes. [4 words]*

Second, they make sentences sound formal and ponderous. For example, the preceding active sentence is conversational; the passive version is not. Third, passive sentences conceal the actor. If you write, "Your product will be shipped," the reader will not know who is handling the shipping. Compare this with "Our Philadelphia office will ship your product." That information might be important to the readers. Finally, passive sentences lack vigor and assertiveness:

Passive: *It was not long before the new assembly routine was mastered by her.*

Active: *She quickly mastered the new assembly routine.*

Most business writing benefits from active *and* passive sentences. The challenge for writers is to find the right balance between them. That balance is determined by the subject matter, the audience, and the writer's goal.

Editing for Accuracy

Once you have done all the preceding steps, you are ready for the final step—editing for accuracy. At this stage, you'll be looking for typos and grammatical errors, misstatements of fact, and vague or ambiguous passages. Before doing this, however, it's often smart to put your written document aside for a while and attend to something else. This break will help you see your writing with fresh eyes when you return to it. Even better, enlist a reliable third party to troubleshoot the piece for you. Even the best of writers benefit from objective editors.

Spelling and Grammatical Errors

Spelling and grammatical errors lead the list of the little nits that plague business writing. Both detract from the power of the message and the authority of the author. Spelling errors are generally the result of careless typing and are easily remedied through diligent proofreading. Grammatical errors have many origins and are more difficult to identify and fix.

SPELLING Check carefully for spelling errors. Yes, your word processor has a spell checker. But don't rely on it to find all your mistakes; it's not that smart. Your spell checker will, for example, judge each of these incorrectly worded sentences to be correct:

Get it right the first thyme.

Get it write the first time.

Got it right the first times.

Considering these shortcomings of the spell checker, you should check every sentence carefully. When in doubt about a particular word spelling or usage, look it up in the dictionary.

AGREEMENT Since a treatise on grammar is beyond the scope of this book, here we treat only one of the more common sources of grammatical errors: agreement. A frequent source of grammatical errors, agreement refers to the correspondence between the elements of a sentence that indicate number, person, gender, or tense. For example, if a sentence has a plural subject, its verb and related words must also be plural:

Although two auditors *[plural] were sent to handle the job,* they *[plural] failed to complete* their *[plural] task on schedule.*

Notice that *auditors, they,* and *their* are all plural words. They are in agreement. Now consider a tricker example:

The problem with all these suggestions is *their lack of consideration of funding.*

Some people would have written:

The problem with all these suggestions are *the lack of consideration of funding.*

What's wrong here? *Are* is a plural verb and agrees with *suggestions,* a plural noun. Unfortunately, *suggestions* is not the subject. *Problem* is the subject—a singular word—and the verb number should agree with it.

Agreement in tense assures that action words (verbs) correspond in terms of past, present, and future. Tenses must agree both within sentences and between them. A frequent mistake of business writers is shifting incorrectly between tenses:

Wrong: *Maria will meet with the audit team next week to discuss our treatment of equipment depreciation. Together, they determine the right method and report it to management. [Look at the verbs to see what's wrong. Here,* will meet *is in the future tense, yet* determine *is in present tense.]*

Right: *Maria will meet with the audit team next week to discuss our treatment of equipment depreciation. Together they will determine the right method and [will] report it to management.*

Misstatements of Fact

Few business writers aim to deceive their readers, but many do so when they fail to check for factual errors or misstatements. Credibility suffers when these gaffs are discovered.

Tip for Catching Those Last Errors

Before you send out your written work, consider having another party check it over. A second pair of eyes will bring a fresh perspective that you, as the author, lack. For example, a sentence whose meaning is clear to you may be ambiguous to someone else. Also, if you've always spelled the name of Michigan's state capital L-a-n-d-s-i-n-k, you won't catch your error in proofing the final copy. Someone else will very likely spot this error.

Numerical errors are the easiest to make. It's very easy to write 5 percent when you mean to write 0.5 percent or 50 percent. It's even easier to misstate a number or percentage when it's in a long table of large numbers. Because the writer is usually copying these numbers from a primary source, keyboard slips are easy to make.

So take the extra time to check all your figures. If you're trying to build a case with your document, even a small error caught by readers will weaken it. They will naturally wonder, "If this part is wrong, what about the rest?"

Summing Up

This chapter has explained four steps you should take to turn a written draft into a polished piece that you can send to others with confidence:

- **Editing for content:** This activity requires that you examine the structure, logic, and message of your draft. Make whatever changes you must to give the draft an attention-stopping beginning, a middle section that logically lays out your message, and an ending that either drives your key point home or urges your reader to action.

- **Editing for style:** A writing style can be forceful, passive, personal, impersonal, colorful, or colorless. Examples of each were given. The style that is right for any particular piece of business writing should be determined by the situation, your relationship with the reader, and the goal you hope to accomplish.

- **Tightening and sharpening sentences:** There's probably no written draft that cannot be improved through these editing activities. Remember that every word and every sentence should add value for the reader. Those that don't should be eliminated. Here are a few summary points to remember: Don't use words that your readers may not understand; give your sentences a logical structure—and don't allow them to be too long. Sentences written in the active voice are usually stronger (and almost always shorter) than passive sentences.

- **Editing for accuracy:** A written document is a reflection on its author. For this reason, as you make a final editorial pass, double-check for typos, ambiguous statements, misspellings, and errors of fact. Look too for grammatical gaffs, particularly errors in agreement, number, person, gender, and tense. As an extra precaution, have someone else put his or her eyes on your edited work. This person may very well see something you've missed.

5

Everyday Writing

Memos, Letters, and E-mail

Key Topics Covered in This Chapter

- *Effective memos*

- *Business letters that do the job*

- *Making the most of e-mail*

N OW THAT we've been through the basics of good writing, we can move on to the particular forms of writing that engage people on a daily basis. For most people, everyday writing consists of memos, letters, and e-mail. Everything we've said up to this point about general principles, drafting, and editing applies to these forms. However, each type of writing has unique characteristics, formats, and other issues you should consider.

Writing Effective Memos

The memo—short for memorandum—is the most common form of *intra*-organizational communication.[1] (If your message is targeted to individuals outside the organization, a letter on company stationery is generally a better format.) A memo may be just a paragraph or two, or it may run on for several pages. You might send a memo to a single recipient or to dozens of people. Still other memos may be included on a "cc" (carbon copy) list. They may be communicated via paper or e-mail.

Memos have many purposes. You can use a memo to announce the hiring or departure of personnel, to issue a new policy, to report on certain activities, to give instructions, to remind people about things they must do, and so forth.

Circulating information by memo has certain advantages for companies and for the people who write them. Unlike verbal communications, memos

- create a record that may be useful in the future,

- allow for detailed reporting,

- give recipients time to think about the content and return to it as necessary,

- facilitate broad distribution.

Like all successful communication tools, a first-class memo involves each of the elements of good writing described in the previous chapters. In this section, we will concentrate on four elements as they relate to the memo: planning, format, execution, and testing.

Planning

The first step in preparing a memo is to define your purpose and your relationship to the addressee or addressees. Keep in mind that although your memo may be directed to an individual or a small group, it may be circulated to a larger audience than you originally envisioned, from your boss's boss to all the employees in your organization.

In her *Guide to Managerial Communication*, Mary Munter describes a useful strategic starting point for deciding on the purpose of your memo.[2] Your purpose may be to tell, to sell, to consult, or to join in. You must understand your purpose before you set down a single word:

- **Tell** when you are in complete command of the necessary authority and information. For example, you're asking a subordinate to carry out a routine task or you're reporting standard information, such as monthly sales figures, to the boss.

- **Sell** when you're in command of the information, but your audience retains the ultimate decision-making power. For example, you're asking other members of the team to buy into your idea.

- **Consult** when you're trying to build consensus toward a given course of action. For example, you're adding your opinion to a multiparty proposal to top management.

- **Join in** when your point of view is one among many. For example, you're serving as a representative to an interdepartmental strategy session and providing background to other participants.

Successful communication of your thoughts stands or falls on taking the proper approach to your audience. Having analyzed your situation, you're ready to write.

Format

Companies generally have a standard memo format. Take a look at those that come your way if you have any questions about what's right at your place of business. In general, memos take this format:

Date: 26 June 2003
To: Jacqueline Whitman
cc: Joe Schwartz, Helen Brown, Max Moreno, Silvia Verde
From: Guy Wordsmith
Subject: New AcmeCorp memo format

One thing to take note of here is the *subject line*. A good writer uses this line to capture the reader's attention and to describe the memo's general contents. In the example, the word *new* is likely to catch people's attention; people are generally alert to the changes that *new* implies. The words *memo format* indicate the contents. Recipients appreciate knowing the contents of a memo right up front. They can then decide if they should read it right away, read it on the train home that night, file it, or fling it. To appreciate the importance of the subject line, consider alternatives to the one just given:

Memos (This could mean anything.)

New format (New format for what?)

New memo format (This is better, but whose format is it?)

The subject line should clearly indicate the purpose and content of your memo. None of these do the job as well as "New AcmeCorp memo format."

Execution

Nothing puts your competence and credibility on the line more than a written document. Say something stupid or inappropriate over the phone or one-on-one, and only one person will hear it. A record of your gaff is highly unlikely. A written document is much different. Several people may see the piece, which may become part of the record. If the document is disorganized, unclear, full of unsupported arguments, and riddled with errors, readers will think of *you* as disorganized, a weak thinker, superficial, and misinformed. For these reasons, never send out a memo under your name until it has been edited to your satisfaction. Edit your initial draft to achieve clear structure, accuracy, clarity of thought and expression, brevity, and vigor. In this way, you can be assured that your memo will accomplish what you set out to do.

CLEAR STRUCTURE The purpose of your memo should be clear by the end of the first sentence, for example, "This memo outlines our goals for the following year and identifies how we intend to achieve them." The rest of the first paragraph should clearly outline the upcoming argument or information. The body of the memo should build on this paragraph by providing the information as succinctly as possible or by organizing the facts that build to your conclusion. The memo should end with specific steps that will lead to the achievement of your goal. If your memo runs on for a full page or more, use headings, bullets, numbered lists, or a combination of these to break up the text and make it more easily skimmed.

ACCURACY When you write to an audience, you are implicitly seeking trust. If even one member of your audience recognizes a factual error, you're in trouble. Inaccuracy in business typically takes these forms: insufficient data, misinterpretation of the data, ignorance of key factors, unconscious bias, and exaggeration. Guard against all these threats to accuracy, to preserve and enhance your credibility.

CLARITY OF THOUGHT AND EXPRESSION Misunderstandings, ambiguity, and confusion cost money and create frustration. Clarity of communication is the antidote. Clear business writing requires clarity of thinking and expression on your part, particularly when you are giving instructions or explaining new policies. To achieve clarity of written expression, you must first achieve clarity of thought. For this reason, you must get your thoughts organized first. Then, once you've set them down on paper, shift your attention to clarity of expression. Your writing will be clear when you edit for content and style, as described in chapter 4.

BREVITY Good memos accomplish much in a few words. Whether your communication is going to the CEO, a junior executive, or hourly employees, brevity is a cardinal virtue. Everyone's time is valuable. Brevity does not mean writing exclusively in short sentences or omitting necessary detail. It means making every word count.

VIGOR Vigorous memos are vivid and memorable. They stand out from the clutter of information and messages that busy people must contend with each day. You can make your memos more vigorous through the use of active voice, nonbureaucratic terms, and short, right-to-the-point sentences. Consider the following two sentences:

> **Corporate–speak (lacks vigor):** *We plan to devote considerable effort to the study of developing product line requirements and potentialities and will seek to share our findings with you and others at a particular future date.*

> **Vigorous:** *We will present our recommendations for product line expansion on November 1.*

The corporate-speak example says almost nothing and is bound to be ignored. The vigorous statement will be read and remembered. It takes a third of the space, sticks in the mind, and conveys much more useful information.

Testing

If you've written a particularly important memo, consider testing it against a representative audience member or two before sending it, especially if it's likely to be widely circulated. Contact these test subjects after the memo has been received, to ask a few important questions:

- Is the memo clear?

- Is more information or explanation required?

- Does it have the right tone? Will anyone take offense?

Testing is particularly important when a memo conveys bad news and when organizational diplomacy is essential. If you don't have anyone to act as your sounding board, set your memo aside for a day. When you revisit it, read it from the perspective of your audience, answering each of the three preceding questions. Make modifications as needed.

Every aspect of a successful memo—its language, accuracy, appropriateness, impact, and result—will affect your success and reputation as a manager. An obvious but important corollary is this: Keep an accurate file of your memos so that you can check long-term results. Refer to your memos when necessary, and build a record of your good work.

Business Letters That Do the Job

Unlike a memo, a business letter is written on the organization's stationery and is typically addressed to an external audience such as a customer, supplier, shareholder, or government agency. Here again, all the principles of good writing apply: an understanding of your readers, a logical structure, an appropriate style, brevity, accuracy, clarity, and so forth. Still, a letter has some unique characteristics you need to consider: format, structure, and what we'll call the goodwill effect.

Format

Business letters in the United States generally adhere to the format shown in figure 5-1. Most parts of a business letter are self-explanatory, but a few bear further discussion.

A greeting is your personal salutation to the reader. If you have a first-name relationship with the reader, use a familiar greeting,

FIGURE 5-1

Sample Business Letter Format

Organizational letterhead	**Gizmo Products Company** **320 Mountain Street** **Hilltop, Arizona 45678** **Phone: (444) 555-6789 Fax: (444) 555-2456** **E-mail: gizmoproducts@wildfire.net** **www.gizmoproducts.com**
Date	June 30, 2003
Recipient's name and address	Mr. Richard Wilson 2 Irving Street Chicago Heights, Illinois 60411
Greeting	Dear Mr. Wilson:
Body	Thank you for ordering our Model 5 Bass Ketcher. We regret that this item is temporarily out of stock because of extraordinary demand. However, Model 5 will be back in stock by the end of this month, at which time we will fill your order, using two-day express shipping at no additional charge. If this is satisfactory, no action is needed on your part. If you wish to cancel your order, please call us at (800) 555-BASS and Gizmo Products will give you a full refund. In either case, I have enclosed a reprint from *Bassaholic Monthly*, which describes the most effective ways to use the Model 5 Bass Ketcher. Good fishing!
Closing	Respectfully,
Signature	*Lisa Goodrich*
Name and title of sender	Lisa Goodrich Director of Customer Care
Additional information (typist's initials, enclosures, "cc" list, etc.)	ral Enclosure

such as "Dear Richard." To do otherwise would seem strange to the recipient. In all other cases, a formal greeting is mandatory: "Dear Mr. Wilson."

Women should be addressed *Ms.* unless they have asked to be addressed otherwise. If the recipient has a known title or rank, such as *Dr.* or *Captain*, then this title has priority over general titles such as *Mr.* or *Ms.*

Often, the exact recipient of a letter is unknown to its author. For example, you may be writing a complaint letter to a company or are submitting a résumé in response to a job advertisement. In those cases, you can use something like these:

Dear Customer Service:

Dear Human Resources Department:

Dear Sir or Madam:

Alternatively, you can eliminate the greeting entirely in favor of an *Attention* line, which directly follows the recipient's address:

Gizmo Products Company
320 Mountain Street
Hilltop, Arizona 45678

Attention: Customer Service

The body of the letter contains your message. Like all good writing, the body should be structured in a way that the message will be read and have the desired effect. In most cases, this means starting with a single sentence or brief paragraph that identifies your purpose for writing or that provides a reference or context for the message itself:

Thank you for ordering our Model 5 Bass Ketcher.

Thank you for applying for the financial analyst position recently advertised in the Herald.

In reference to your advertisement for an experienced financial analyst . . .

I am writing to report a defect in a shirt purchased through your catalog.

Once you've established the reason for your writing, or the context, you can get into the meat of your message. Give that message a logical structure. Be clear. Be brief. And check to be sure that you've included all the information the recipient will need in responding.

After you have delivered the message, write a closing statement that either wraps it up or indicates the response you expect from the reader:

I would appreciate your sending the replacement part by overnight mail.

Please contact me directly if I can be of further assistance.

Best wishes with your job search.

We look forward to your decision.

The Goodwill Factor

Every letter represents an opportunity to create goodwill for your organization, even when you must report bad news to the recipient, as in these cases:

We cannot approve your loan.

Your shipment will be delayed.

The book you ordered is no longer in print.

Someone else has been selected for the job.

Your child is not sufficiently prepared to enter Elite Prep School.

Reporting bad news could jeopardize an important relationship with the recipient. For example, an individual who has maintained checking and savings accounts with a bank for many years may not receive approval on a business start-up loan. The bank has a strong

Letter and Memo Wizards

Though most users of the ubiquitous Microsoft Word don't realize it, this word processing program contains handy templates (Word calls them Wizards) for creating letters and memos. You can locate them under File/New. These templates take you step-by-step through a process that allows you to select a particular page design and document style, and create a preferred heading. They will also prompt you to add other elements such as an attention or a subject line, the typist's initials, and enclosures. Once the steps are completed, you have created a letter or memo template that you can quickly return to and use with other correspondence.

interest in keeping that person's business, even though its lending policies are likely to disappoint this customer. The bank can deliver bad news *and* maintain goodwill if it follows certain practices.

First, you can express your regret in a sincere manner:

Wrong: *We cannot approve your application for a business loan.*

Right: *On behalf of Mountain View Bank, I regret to inform you that we cannot honor your request for a business loan at this time.*

Another way you can maintain goodwill is by giving a reason for the bad news. A reasonable explanation can often neutralize negative feelings. Recognizing positive things about the recipient can do the same:

Like other lending institutions, our bank cannot make loans—even to customers with excellent credit ratings, such as you—if total monthly debt payments exceed a certain percentage of gross monthly income.

Finally, you should keep the door open. In some cases, your bad news may not be final:

Naturally, our lending committee would be glad to reconsider your loan request if something in your financial situation should change: an increase in monthly income, retirement of some current debt, a smaller loan request, or other circumstances.

Making the Most of E-mail

E-mail is the transmission of files or messages through a computer network.[3] When that network is linked to the Internet, employees can communicate with people across the street or on the other side of the world in the blink of an eye.

E-mail is a handy medium for sending memos and notices and for forwarding information received electronically from others. And thanks to the "attachment" capabilities of current browsers, a writer can develop a lengthy document in Microsoft Word or another word processing program and send it to others, saving enormously in time and postage charges.

It's so easy to send an e-mail that, at times, it doesn't seem like writing at all. But e-mail is a form of business correspondence that requires the same kind of attention that memos and letters receive.

E-mail has become the dominant method of communication in most companies. Why? Because it's inexpensive, fast, and easy.

Unfortunately, the speed and ease of e-mail have created some problems for business writers and their companies. First, employees sometimes send and often receive time-wasting, unnecessary messages. Second, many e-mails are sloppily written. People simply write down what's on their minds and hit the "Send" button without reflection on content or composition. Third, emotional and ill-considered messages are sometimes sent before the writer has had time to calm down. Fourth, messages are occasionally misdirected or forwarded to unintended recipients—sometimes with negative consequences. And finally, even deleted e-mails can be retrieved for use in disciplinary proceedings or can be subpoenaed for use in legal disputes. These problems can all be handled through common sense and the application of sound writing principles.

Put Power in the Subject Line

Like the memo subject line, the e-mail subject line should be the lure that gets your reader interested and signals the memo's contents. For this reason, your subject should meet at least one of the following goals:

- Contain your key message: "Sales meeting rescheduled to 2 P.M. on Friday"

- Include the desired action or response: "Your comments urgently needed by 4 P.M. today"

- Be specific but not too long: "How about lunch tomorrow?"

- Allow your reader to file and retrieve your message easily: "John's report"

In contrast, a weak subject line gives little or no information—or too much to be read on one line. If the subject line is too general, vague, or left blank, the reader may skip or delete the message altogether. Remember: Busy people can receive fifty to one hundred e-mail messages per day. To ensure that yours is opened and read, it must stand out.

Use One Message per E-mail

Treat each e-mail as a coherent information packet—to ask a question, communicate your opinion, report news, and so forth. You will achieve coherence if each e-mail contains only one message. If you have more than one message for a recipient, create a separate e-mail for each, and give each a strong, appropriate subject line.

The one-message e-mail has two major advantages: First, the recipient(s) can digest and respond to a single message more easily. Second, if a recipient forwards your e-mail to another party, other messages—which may be highly inappropriate—won't be dragged along, as in the following multimessage e-mail:

Subject: Sales meeting rescheduled to 3 P.M. on Friday

Bill: We've had to reschedule because of Amy's out-of-town trip. Please forward this message to any of your people who are planning to attend.

On another note, I took your advice about shifting some of Karl's responsibilities over to Cynthia. His analytical skills aren't up to speed yet. Thanks for the suggestion.

Can you imagine the consequences of this multimessage e-mail being forwarded to several people in the company? Surely the writer has no intention of sharing his personal view of Karl's skills with Bill's sales colleagues. Clicking the "Forward" button is so easy that gaffs like this are bound to happen when people overload their e-mails with more than one topic.

Tips for E-mail Messaging

E-mail represents a unique communications medium that requires some special safeguards:

- Put the key message in your subject line to lessen the risk of your reader's ignoring or deleting an important message.

- Keep your message short. Try to put all pertinent information on the first screen page.

- Cover only one topic per e-mail.

- Edit and spell-check before sending anything—unless you don't mind looking bad.

- Never send an e-mail message when you're angry. It's easy to do. Ask yourself, "Would I say this to the person's face?" If the answer is no, then don't send the message.

- Add the address as the last step before you click "Send." This reduces the chance that you'll send an unfinished message.

Use Attachments for Long Messages

One of the great benefits of e-mail is the ability to attach other files. In the bad old days, word processing files, spreadsheets, overhead projection pages, and other types of electronic files had to be printed and sent by mail or fax. Today, we can save time and money by simply attaching these files, which arrive in an instant. Best of all, recipients can make changes in these files and send them back with the same speed and convenience.

In addition to the documents just cited, attachments are most appropriate when you are sending long messages and reports. Long messages require lots of annoying on-screen scrolling by the recipient. Also, many special formatting features that we use in lengthy documents (e.g., boldface headings, bullets, footnotes) don't work well in e-mail systems. For this reason, when you have a long message to transmit, send it as an attachment. Then use the e-mail message to inform the reader what the attachment is about and what the reader should do with it.

From: Howard
To: Charlene
Subject: Our Customer Survey Report
Attachment: Survey report.doc

Hello, Charlene:
My first draft of the customer survey report is attached. Please review and return it with your comments.
Thanks,
Howard

Four Elements of E-mail Policy

Despite its great convenience for businesses, e-mail may make a company vulnerable to lawsuits for harassment and libel. Although companies have every right to store and review e-mail messages created by employees on company equipment and on company time, fewer than 40 percent actually do review messages, according to a survey released by the American Management Association in early 2000. Managers are either unconcerned or reluctant to create an Orwellian atmosphere in which people feel they are being watched.

One way to deal with these issues is to create an e-mail policy that is both sensible and explained to all employees.[4] Such a policy has four elements:

1. **Enforce zero tolerance for harassment and discrimination.** An increasing number of sexual and racial harassment lawsuits against companies feature damaging e-mails as evidence: persistent e-mail requests for dates, racy jokes, pornography downloaded from the Internet, and so forth. Make it clear that this type of activity will not be tolerated.

2. **Explain how e-mail is stored.** The informality of e-mail can lull users into a false sense of comfort. If you send or receive something questionable, just hit the delete button and no one will be the wiser, right? Wrong. Deleting merely sends a document into the recesses of your hard drive, where it will remain until the drive is purged. E-mail messages are also stored on the server in a form that makes them retrievable by computer forensic experts. Just knowing that their messages are stored will often prevent most people from abusing the company's e-mail system.

3. **Insist that confidential information be transmitted via another medium.** This may seem like a no-brainer, but lawyers say it's alarming how often employees use e-mail to discuss sensitive matters such as new pricing and their assessment of a senior executive's performance. Make it clear that sensitive matters should be transmitted through more secure media: a confidential memorandum or a one-on-one conversation.

4. **Observe copyright restrictions.** It's easy—too easy—to download copyright-protected software and other materials and then e-mail them to your associates. You can't stop employees from receiving these from their friends, but you can insist that they delete them and not pass them along.

Summing Up

This chapter examined the three most common forms of business writing. Although writers should approach each form using the principles and editing concepts described in earlier chapters, these forms have some unique characteristics worth noting:

- **Memos:** Use these for written communication *within* the organization. Discussion of memos in this chapter focused on planning, format, execution, and testing. The planning of a memo begins with the determination of its purpose. In a large company, a memo's format generally follows an accepted model. All, however, feature a subject line, which you must use effectively if you want to catch the readers' attention.

- **Business letters:** Business letters are similar to memos but are typically for external consumption. We described a standard letter format and offered advice on proper greetings. Additionally, we showed how writers can even use "bad news" letters to generate goodwill. Because letters create an impression about you and your company in the minds of customers, suppliers, job applicants, and other outside parties, you should handle your correspondence in the most thoughtful way possible.

- **E-mail:** This electronic form of communication has quickly become the medium of choice for managers and employees in most sectors of the economy. As described here, however, this medium's fast and easy virtues can create problems for those who send e-mail. One problem is just getting noticed. Because people receive so many e-mails each day, you must use the subject line to make your e-mails both stand out *and* drive your message home. The other take-aways about e-mail are these: Use one message per e-mail; use attachments for long letters; and review what you've written *before* you hit that "Send" button.

6

Presentations

Timeless Principles

Key Topics Covered in This Chapter

- *Presentation structure—the Greek way*

- *Four rhetorical devices*

- *The learning styles of listeners*

- *How to aim for the head and the heart*

PRESENTATIONS are a powerful way to communicate your message to a group. They are opportunities to gather an audience together in one place to tell your story and gather feedback. You can use presentations to persuade the audience to take a particular course of action, to convey information, to gain commitment, or to provide a forum for discussion of controversial or challenging ideas.

As we did for our discussion of written communication in chapter 1, we begin our treatment of presentations with basic principles. The first involves presentation structure—one that goes back to the ancient Greeks. The next major section explains four rhetorical devices you can use to give your presentation greater impact. Another major section explains the learning styles of the typical audience. If you understand these styles and how to address them, then your presentations will be much better received. Finally, the chapter urges presenters to speak not only to the head, but to the heart.

Presentations: The Greek Way

In learning how to make a great presentation, take a cue from the people who did it first and did it well—the ancient Greeks.[1] The Athenian Greeks developed a number of presentation techniques as they began their experiment with democratic government. They quickly realized that in the absence of a king, the people needed a legal system to restrain their fellow citizens. The art of public speaking emerged from the Greek experiment with democracy and the legal system that followed in its wake.

Indeed, the five-part Greek outline for a persuasive speech—introduction, narrative, argument, refutation, and conclusion—has never been significantly improved. Some twenty-five hundred years later, you can use the Greeks' insights to strengthen your own presentations.

The Introduction

Today, the convention wisdom is this: Tell your audience what you are going to say, then say it, and then tell them what you just said. The Greeks did not subscribe to this approach. They found it predictable and boring—and countless audiences have agreed. Audiences quickly figure out what you're up to, and once they do, they listen to one of the three parts of the presentation and ignore the rest. You're left talking to glazed eyes during the other two parts.

The Greeks used the introduction to prepare the audience to hear the speech favorably. Here are a few of their strategies.

TALK ABOUT THE AUDIENCE You can never go wrong complimenting the audience.

It is a pleasure to be with a group that has demonstrated, once again, what sales excellence stands for.

TALK ABOUT THE PREVIOUS SPEAKER If your talk is one of a series, refer to a previous speaker who made a deep impression on the audience.

Jane moved us all with her eloquent appeal to the core values of this company. Now, I'd like to talk to you about a subject I feel as strongly about as Jane feels about company values: cost accounting.

TALK ABOUT THE EVENT Draw the participants' attention to something that is special or unique about the event. Doing so heightens their interest and gives them a happy sense that the occasion is an important one. They'll listen more closely as a result.

This morning you will have the distinct privilege of meeting three of the most important innovators in our industry.

TALK ABOUT A MOMENT IN HISTORY If you can put the time and date of the presentation into a historical context, the audience will derive a greater sense of purpose and gravity than it otherwise would.

Three years ago this week, I stood at this same podium and described to you the desperate financial condition of our company. What a difference three years have made.

TALK ABOUT THE PLACE The hall, the town, the state, or even the country where the presentation takes place is grist for the introductory mill.

This little town, a town that two hundred years ago witnessed the first American stirrings toward freedom and the establishment of a new, democratic country, is today the proud site of the new Greater Lexington Patriot Shopping Mall.

TALK ABOUT THE POINT OF THE SPEECH It is your privilege as the speaker to frame the topic, to create the context for the conversation. Use this to subtly steer the audience away from topics you don't want to discuss, or to refocus the audience on topics with which you are comfortable.

We're here today to talk about our company's profit profile over the past six months. Frankly, it's not very good. But what really lies at the heart of the profit issue is customer satisfaction, and I'd like to spend a little time addressing that.

The Narrative

The essence of the narrative is a story. Here you must get to the heart of the matter, whether it involves something you want your listeners to do, something you wish to convince them of, or something about which you want to tell them. If you don't find yourself phrasing what you have to say in terms of a story, rethink the material. Put the essence of your communication into a story of your devising, one that relates the facts in the way you wish your audience to understand them.

The Argument

In the argument of your presentation, you present the proofs, or supporting logic, for your point. This section is probably the most important part of the presentation for bringing your audience around to your point of view. Remember that audiences recall very little of what they hear. For this reason, keep your factual evidence to the necessary minimum and your main arguments to three or four at the most. More than that will actually weaken your case, because your audience will become exasperated with you and begin to believe that you are trying to bolster a weak argument with every point you can think of.

It is helpful to provide transitional comments throughout this section to help guide your audience through your arguments.

There are three reasons why expansion of the city's nine-hole golf course would be fiscally unsound. First, the course's reported earnings are substantially overstated—perhaps by 50 percent. This is a consequence of amateurish profit-and-loss accounting by the Park Department. Second, there is no adequate water supply. The city is already struggling to meet the water needs of its residents and businesses. And third, the opening of two new golf courses in this county within the past few years has dissipated demand. Revenues from an expanded course will be disappointing.

The Refutation

In the fourth section of the Greek speech model, you anticipate objections to your argument. This section is particularly important when the subject is controversial. You must give a real hearing to opposing points of view, even if you subsequently demolish them with brilliant rhetoric. Failure to do so will cause your audience to complain that you never even considered the opposition. The more explosive the topic, the more important it is to state your opponents' points of view and to do so early in the refutation.

You can handle the refutation in three ways:

1. Answer anticipated rebuttals to your own arguments.

2. Take the opportunity to rehearse and reject your opponents' arguments. Again, this tactic is essential for highly controversial topics.

3. Mix the two approaches.

The Conclusion

The conclusion should not summarize your arguments; rather, it should appeal to the audience for its understanding, its action, and its approval—whatever it is you want the audience to do or think. The Greeks were very clear that a summary was not wanted here. So don't fall into the trap of telling your audience what you said. Doing so will leave them bored and vaguely irritated. Since audiences tend to remember the last thing they've heard, summing up is a surefire way to kill any enthusiasm your presentation may have generated. So forget about a summary; instead, tell your audience what it should think or do.

> *As you leave here today, do so with the confidence that the products you represent are the best on the market, have the strongest service backing, and are priced to provide the greatest value to customers.*

Four Rhetorical Devices

The ancient Greeks didn't simply develop a five-part structure for making a presentation. They also developed rhetorical devices for connecting with audiences—devices that remain highly effective today. These include parallel structure, triads, antithesis, and rhetorical questions.

Parallel Structure

Parallel structure uses sentence elements that are alike in both function and construction. Parallel structure is especially useful in presentations because the repetition of language structure helps audiences hear and remember what we have to say. Consider Churchill's speech on Dunkirk to the House of Commons, 4 June 1940:

> *We shall not flag or fail. We shall go on to the end. We shall fight in France. We shall fight on the seas and oceans. We shall fight with growing confidence and growing strength in the air. We shall defend our island, whatever the cost may be. We shall fight on the beaches. We shall fight on the landing grounds. We shall fight in the fields and in the streets. We shall fight in the hills; we shall never surrender.*

You can use similar language structure to good effect in business situations: "We will work hard. We will work smart. We will create a better future for the company and for ourselves."

Triads

The Greeks noticed early on that people are attracted to lists of three items. Call it the Rule of Threes or simply a *triad*. A group of three seems to our minds complete and satisfying. No one is quite sure why. The end of Martin Luther King's famous "I Have a Dream" speech illustrates the use of triads. He liked them so much that he gave his audience a double dose:

When we let freedom ring, when we let it ring from every village and every hamlet, from every state and every city, we will be able to speed up that day when all of God's children, black men and white men, Jews and Gentiles, Protestants and Catholics, will be able to join hands and sing in the words of the old Negro spiritual, Free at last! Free at last! Thank God Almighty, we are free at last!

You can use triads to good effect in any number of business presentations:

Our new reflective window film will reduce your air-conditioning costs, eliminate annoying glare, and protect your furnishings from sun damage.

The new strategy will work if we do our job as managers. That means articulating our goals, making sure that every employee understands how his or her job fits with the strategy, and aligning rewards with the right behavior at every level.

Antithesis

In rhetoric, *antithesis* is the placing of a sentence or one of its parts in opposition to another to capture the listener's attention or to evoke a strong response. Consider, for example, the motto of the state of New Hampshire: Live Free or Die.

Antithesis is rarely used today, even though it is an elegant form of expression and one that people remember vividly. Consider the ending of President Kennedy's inaugural address in January 1961. The entire speech was laced with antithesis, but the ending had particular potency because it talked directly to the audience:

And so, my fellow Americans, ask not what your country can do for you; ask what you can do for your country.

Because of its dramatic effect, antithesis is less available to the business speaker. Still you may find opportunities:

The choice is ours. We can live with the defender's dilemma, or grasp the innovator's advantage.

Rhetorical Questions

Rhetorical questions are questions asked for the sole purpose of producing an effect on the audience. The speaker does not expect his or her questions to be answered—least of all by the audience.

Rhetorical questions draw listeners into the topic because they call for answers, even if they are not uttered out loud. Consider Patrick Henry's famous speech of March 1775, on the eve of the American revolution:

> *Gentlemen may cry, "Peace! Peace!" but there is no peace. The war is actually begun! The next gale that sweeps from the north will bring to our ears the clash of resounding arms! Our brethren are already in the field! Why stand we here idle? What is it that gentlemen wish? What would they have? Is life so dear, or peace so sweet, as to be purchased at the price of chains and slavery?*

Having posed his rhetorical questions, Henry answered them in the strongest terms:

> *Forbid it, Almighty God! I know not what course others may take, but as for me, give me liberty, or give me death!*

Note the antithesis in Patrick Henry's last sentence.

As a businessperson, you have ample opportunities for posing rhetorical questions and then stating your reply to them. Consider this example:

> *If we keep on following the same ineffective strategy, this company can expect shrinking market share and declining profitability. Do you want to work for a company like that? Are you comfortable with mediocrity? I think not. That's why I have offered this plan, and why I'm here today to ask for your support.*

Three Learning Styles

Another point to remember as you develop and present your ideas is that different audience members are likely to have different primary styles of learning.[2] You may be familiar with the three learning styles, typically referred to as visual, auditory, and kinesthetic. Most people are strong in one of these styles and weaker in the others.

- **Visual learners:** These learners respond best to pictures, graphs, and other visual stimuli. Research shows that 30 to 40 percent of people are visual learners.

- **Auditory learners:** As you may have guessed, these people are more responsive to words and other sounds. An estimated 20 to 30 percent of the population are auditory learners.

- **Kinesthetic learners:** This type of person is most engaged by physical activities: handling a prototype, working at a laboratory bench, or watching a presenter who moves around, mingles with the audience, or uses props. Some 30 to 50 percent of people are kinesthetic learners.

If you want to get the attention of these different types of learners, and get them to respond to what you have to say, then your presentation must be couched in their learning modes. Otherwise you'll lose your audience. This adaptation to learning style is easier said than done, since we can never be certain as to the preferred style of a particular audience. Moreover, any audience is bound to contain a mixture of visual, auditory, and kinesthetic learners. The best way to deal with these issues is to provide something for everyone—some blend of visual, auditory, and kinesthetic styles.

To appreciate how this different style might be employed, consider this fairly typical business presentation. One of your colleagues is reporting the last quarter's results. She stands in front of the group, turns on the overhead projector or her computer, and cues up the first slide. A sea of words and numbers greets your weary eyes. She then launches into reading every word on the screen. You shift in your chair, trying to get comfortable. As slide after slide winks by and your colleague continues to drone on in a flat voice, you gradually sink into a semistupor. At the end, you shake yourself awake and exit the meeting room wondering, "What was that about?"

Now, here's how the three learning styles could be applied to this doleful scene.

Add a dose of visual learning. Like most presenters, your colleague thinks she has appealed to the visual learners by using slides. But most business slides are covered border to border with words, when what visual learners need is pictures—preferably, simple pictures. So, connect your key concepts visually to angles, circles, squares, and the like. Don't get fancy. It's simply not necessary, and it doesn't promote learning. In addition to pictures, you can use tables and other graphic illustrations for variety—but keep in mind that simpler is usually better.

Cue up your auditory learners. You reach auditory learners through talk—but certain kinds of talk work better than others. Storytelling is one. Parables and anecdotes appeal to auditory learners and are often memorable. In addition, you can employ discussion groups, debates, question-and-answer sessions, and the like—anything that will get you talking in ways more connected to a story than the usual discursive style of business presentation.

Add liveliness through kinesthetic learning. Kinesthetic learners may be the most often neglected people at business presentations. Much of what goes on in the business world appeals to the head, not the body, and presentations are rarely exceptions to this dismal rule. The key here is to get your listeners to do something. Get them involved early and often through role-playing, games, working with models, even creating charts and physical representations of what you want them to learn. For example, you can increase your listeners' energy enormously at the opening of a speech simply by having them stand up and shout something appropriate or fun. It's corny, but it works. That's because you have appealed to the kinesthetics in the audience.

Use all three of these learning modes in a presentation, and your audience will pay great attention and remember more.

Aim for the Head *and* the Heart

One more technique to engaging the audience deserves mention here: doing something to engage the emotions. Though not always appropriate to the situation, an emotional approach, when the situation warrants it, can be a powerful tool for getting people on the side of your ideas.

Our business culture has a decided slant toward the analytical and cerebral. So it's not surprising that many presenters—and business writers—concentrate on the logic of their arguments and quantitative supporting evidence. An emotional component isn't there or, if it is, is not recognized. In making a case for the development of a new product, for example, presenters inevitably roll out lots of products specs, pro forma financial statements, and other numerical fireworks. All this information aims for the head.

Many business issues, however, have unstated personal and emotional components. Though they are not discussed, these components may exert substantial power over listeners. Consider a new product-line concept as an example. On the surface, it's all about potential revenues, cost estimates, marketing issues, and good fit with company strategy. Beneath the surface, however, the new product line may affect individual listeners in important ways, including the following:

> **As a threat:** *If that new product line performs as predicted, the importance of my product line will be overshadowed.*
>
> **As an opportunity to benefit personally:** *If this thing works, our annual bonuses will triple. I could help my kids pay off their college loans, or I could retire earlier than planned.*
>
> **As a change in the workplace:** *If it worked as planned, that new product line would make a big difference around here. We wouldn't always be worried about layoffs and budget cuts. People would enjoy coming to work for a change.*

A good presentation recognizes these types of emotion-laden concerns. The presenter speaks to the head *and* the heart. In doing

How King Harry Said It

In Shakespeare's *Henry V*, the young king and his small army found themselves in a desperate spot near a French village called Agincourt. Out of food and weak with dysentery, they faced annihilation by an overwhelming enemy force.

Had Henry followed the usual presentation formula, he would have spoken to the heads of his dispirited troops, describing the tactical situation, how the French would most likely deploy against them, and how they should act.

> *Here's the situation, team: The relative strengths are one to five in their favor. The French strategy, as shown on the slate chalkboard held by Lord Gloucester, will be to break our front with a direct assault of mounted knights.*
>
> *Our strategy will be for the archers to break up their charge, with the men-at-arms rushing out to dispatch or capture the fallen. All ransoms collected will go to the profit-sharing fund. So, go now to your preassigned positions, and whatever you do, don't run away!*

But Shakespeare's Henry spoke to his men's hearts instead of their heads. In one of the greatest pep talks ever penned, the king reminded his men of their bonds of brotherhood and described a future in which their deeds and sacrifices would be remembered and honored.

> *This day is called the feast of Crispian:*
> *He that outlives this day, and comes safe home,*
> *Will stand a tip-toe when the day is named,*
> *And rouse him at the name of Crispian.*
> *He that shall live this day, and see old age,*
> *Will yearly on the vigil feast his neighbours,*
> *And say "Tomorrow is Saint Crispian":*
> *Then will he strip his sleeve and show his scars.*
> *And say "These wounds I had on Crispin's day."*

Continued

> *Old men forget: yet all shall be forgot,*
> *But he'll remember with advantages*
> *What feats he did that day: then shall our names,*
> *Familiar in his mouth as household words,*
> *Harry the king, Bedford and Exeter,*
> *Warwick and Talbot, Salisbury and Gloucester,*
> *Be in their flowing cups freshly remember'd.*
> *This story shall the good man teach his son;*
> *And Crispin Crispian shall ne'er go by,*
> *From this day to the ending of the world,*
> *But we in it shall be remember'd;*
> *We few, we happy few, we band of brothers . . .* [3]

so, he or she engages listeners at a deeper level. Consequently, once you've presented the intellectual side of your story, shift to its deeper personal meaning for the audience. And use personal pronouns to signal your shift from cold-blooded objectivity:

> *That concludes our presentation of the revenue and cost estimates for the proposed product line. We have confidence in those estimates and the long-term profits they point to.*
>
> *We believe, too, that this product line has the power to change our company in fundamental ways—and much for the better. If you're tired of apologizing for our outdated designs and technology, these new products will restore your pride in what we stand for. If you're tired of being a market follower, these products will make us the market innovator and the company that our customers look to for technical leadership.*

Did you notice all the personal pronouns in that ending: *we, you, you're, our*? Don't lay it on too thick, but speak to the hearts of your listeners if it's appropriate to the situation and if you want to make a real impression.

In some cases, speaking to the heart means telling listeners what's in it for them. If you do this, frame the material you're presenting from the audience's point of view. Why should they care about the topic at hand? Give them a compelling reason and you'll have their attention.

Summing Up

- The Greek approach to public speaking involves a five-part structure: the introduction, narrative, argument, refutation, and conclusion. The same structure can be used today for organizing and delivering business speeches and presentations. The *introduction* prepares the audience to be receptive. The *narrative* is the part in which the speaker tells his or her story. In the *argument*, the speaker presents supporting logic. The speaker then uses *refutation* to anticipate and rebut possible objections to his or her position. The *conclusion* appeals to the audience for acceptance or some particular action.

- The four rhetorical devices used by the Greeks to connect with and convince their listeners are parallel structure, triads, antithesis, and rhetorical questions. These devices are as useful today as they were ages ago.

- The three primary learning styles of listeners—visual, auditory, and kinesthetic—were described in this chapter. Presenters should adjust their talks to the known learning style of their audiences. When the style is mixed or unknown, the speaker should include something for everyone.

- Presenters should aim not merely for the heads of their listeners, but also for their hearts. Many business situations—but not all—have unstated personal or emotional components. When these are present, speakers should factor them into their talks. Doing so will engage listeners at a deeper level and produce a better outcome.

Backstage

Preparing Your Presentation

Key Topics Covered in This Chapter

- *Defining your objective*

- *Understanding the audience*

- *Deciding what to say*

- *Getting organized*

- *Developing effective visuals*

- *Rehearsing*

CHAPTER 6 described time-tested principles that you can use as a foundation for your presentations. This chapter moves from principles to six practical steps you can take in preparing those presentations.[1]

Step 1: Define Your Objective

The objective of your presentation is the outcome you seek—shared information, discussion, buy-in, feedback, or a sale, for example. It drives the development of your presentation. Ask yourself, "Why am I making this presentation, and what do I want my audience to do as a result?"

Do you want to inform, persuade, or sell? Do you want the audience to understand, learn, or take action? Do you want commitment from the audience? Note the difference between presenting a budget so that your audience understands it and presenting a budget so that your audience will vote in favor of it. The objective of the first is to inform; the second is to persuade. Once you are clear about the objective, you will have a better idea about the following issues:

- Whether to give the presentation at all

- Whether to give it to this particular audience under these particular circumstances

- What to say and how to say it

- What the follow-up needs to be

- Possible objections

Step 2: Understand the Audience

A presentation creates a connection between you and your audience. The better you understand that audience, the more you can customize your presentation, making it more appealing and effective in its impact. Everything we said about understanding the audience in the chapters on writing applies here:

- Who are your audience members, and what is their relationship to the topic?

- How well informed are they about the subject? What do they need to know about it?

- What do they expect from the presentation?

You should also determine if the audience is accustomed to a certain type of presentation. For example, all the sales personnel in a stock brokerage office were accustomed to a twenty-minutes sales briefing every Monday morning. They expected to receive practical ideas about timely investments or news about new stock and bond issues that would be available in the coming week. They were annoyed by speakers who went beyond twenty minutes or who failed to convey commission-producing ideas or information.

In addition to establishing what your audience knows about the subject, you should determine what the audience knows about you and what more they need to know. If you understand your audience's level of knowledge, then you'll know how much of your presentation must be devoted to your own introduction and your standing on the subject. You should also determine how the audience feels about you and your subject. Are they likely to be enthusiastic? Polite? Apathetic? Hostile? A hostile or apathetic audience must be handled with care. A securities analyst whose recent stock recommendations had been lousy considered his audience of stock-brokers carefully before he returned to face them. Many were upset, since his advice had encouraged them to promote a number of losing stocks to their clients. The analyst used humor to diffuse those bad feelings. "As I stand before you this morning," he began, "I feel like the Olympic javelin thrower who has just won the coin toss and elected to receive." That statement got plenty of laughs and helped diffuse the anger of many brokers.

Step 3: Decide What to Say

Many of us have experienced the paralysis of knowing what we want to accomplish, but having trouble putting down the actual words and ideas. One approach is to break the task into three parts.

Tips on Reviewing the Content of Your Presentation

As you review the content of your presentation, make sure of the following:

- Your key message supports the objectives of the presentation.

- The arguments you have marshaled are well developed and understandable to all members of the audience.

- The content will convince the audience to agree with you.

- Contrary arguments are effectively neutralized.

Remember: Include only those details that will persuade. If you are not sure about the impact of a particular detail, leave it out.

---

1. Define your key message, that is, what you want people to remember and what action you want them to take. This message flows directly from your objective. You can have a number of supporting arguments, ideas, and facts, but only one key message.

2. Next, identify the arguments that best support your message. Avoid excessive detail, but be sure to talk about more than *just* the facts. It is important to identify and address the emotional underpinnings of your message. Why should the audience care about it?

3. Finally, identify at which point you need audience participation, agreement, or buy-in.

After you have generated your initial set of ideas on what to say, you are ready to review and refine them.

Step 4: Get Organized

Once you have the raw material for your presentation, you need to organize it. A well-organized presentation will make the audience's listening job easier, boosting the likelihood that you will accomplish your objective.

As described in chapter 6, the ancient Greeks saw the ideal presentation as having five parts: the introduction, the narrative, the argument, the refutation (of competing ideas), and the conclusion. What worked then works today, but modern presenters favor a similar but slightly truncated version of four parts: the opening, the problem (or need), the solution, and the action step.

During the opening, use a "hook"—a comment, a question, a relevant story, a statement, or an example—to get your audience's interest and attention. Additionally, use the opening to do the following:

- Define the purpose of the presentation.

- Establish your credibility. Ask yourself, "Which of my credentials will impress this particular audience?" and emphasize those. Or, if appropriate, have another person with authority or credibility introduce your presentation.

- Describe the importance of the topic for the audience. Explain what's in it for them.

- Preview very briefly the main points to be covered.

The second part of your presentation is the need or problem statement. Here you should accomplish several tasks:

- Make it clear to the audience members why they should care about your message.

- Develop a clear need or problem that you and the audience will solve together. Incorporate relevant arguments, examples, and a variety of supporting material to sustain interest without distracting from the point.

- Involve the audience by asking for their suggestions and addressing their needs and issues.

- Test acceptance by periodically asking for feedback.

The solution, the third part of your presentation, explains to the audience how you think the problem should be solved or the need satisfied. Here you will help the audience visualize the benefits of the solution. As you do so, phrase your solution in terms of the audience's needs, and make sure that your solution matches those needs.

In the fourth and final step of your presentation, you wrap up with a strong call to action. This call requires you to take several steps:

- Reiterate the presentation's key message.

- Integrate your opening points into your closing comments.

- Recommend action.

Tips on Adding Interest

To keep your audience's interest level high, incorporate some of the following visual, verbal, and physical techniques:

Variety in pitch, time, speed, and body language	Illustrations
	Expert testimony
Personal stories	Statistics
Analogies	Charts and graphs
Humor	Audience involvement
Examples	Personal energy and eye contact
Quotes	

- Suggest agreement.

- Obtain commitment or buy-in.

- Provide closure.

Whatever you do, don't use the action step to summarize what you've already said. That's boring and will rob you of an opportunity to advance your agenda. Instead, use the ending to thrust your point home. Give the audience something to do with information you've now imparted. As John F. Kennedy told listeners at the conclusion of his inaugural address, "Ask not what your country can do for you; ask what you can do for your country." Few of us get the chance to ask our audiences to do something that exciting, but we do owe them our best efforts toward real action, because audiences tend to remember what comes last in a presentation.

Step 5: Develop Effective Visuals

As described in chapter 6, everyone has a preferred learning style, but most people respond better to visuals than to the spoken word alone. Research has shown that 75 percent of what people know is acquired visually. In addition, a picture is three times more effective

FIGURE 7-1

Triangle Visual Aid

in conveying information than words alone. Words and pictures together *are six times* more effective than words alone.

You can use visual aids to help your audience maintain attention, remember facts, and understand ideas or physical layouts. Visuals can also be used to signal your listeners that you are moving on to a new topic. For example, if your presentation involves three related points—sales, service, and follow-up—you can arrange these around the points of a triangle. Then when you move from one to the other, the point you're discussing could be highlighted in the next slide (figure 7-1). In the figure, the boldface and boxed "Service" indicates that this topic will now be taken up. The technical capabilities of presentation software allow for even more eye-catching formatting.

Remember, however, that when the audience is looking at a visual, it is not looking at you so keep visuals to a minimum. Moreover, do not use a lot of word slides as a speaker's outline; instead, know your speech thoroughly.

You have many choices for your visuals, including overheads, slides, PC-based slides, flip charts, and handouts. When selecting from among these media, consider their pros and cons (table 7-1).

Effective visuals share two virtues: simplicity and clarity. Nothing is less helpful than a slide crammed border to border with either text or complex graphics. For this reason, use key words

TABLE 7-1

The Pros and Cons of Different Media

Medium	Pros	Cons
Overheads	Flexible	Can be awkward putting up and switching between overheads
	Easy to create	
	Can allow light in the room for continued eye contact	
	Good for both formal and informal situations	
Slides	Easy to create	Take time to produce
	Good for formal presentations	Require a darkened room and allow for minimal eye contact
PC-Based Slides	Easy to create, to update, and to transport	Do not always project clearly
		Technology can break down, necessitating a backup set of overhead slides
Flip Charts	Encourage interaction	Not effective for large groups
	Flexible	Difficult to transport
	Easy to create	
Handouts	Can contain supplemental background information	Can become the audience's focal point, distracting them from listening to you
	Useful for informal, short presentations	(Avoid handing out reading material during the presentation. It detracts from your presentation.)
	Provide a place for note-taking and a take-away for later reference	

instead of full sentences and paragraphs, as in the following example, and limit the number of ideas you present on any one visual.

Our Value Proposition to Customers

- *Quality materials and workmanship*

- *Reasonable price*

- *Unmatched service*

When you use graphic images, reduce them to their essentials. A good graphic is practically self-explanatory. If you find that you

Tips on Using Visuals

Visuals are effective partners if you use them for certain tasks:

Open: Help your audience focus on the purpose of the presentation.

Present the agenda: List the key elements of what is to come.

Highlight key points: Use memorable words and phrases, or illustrate points with charts or graphs.

Review a structured process: Analyze the whole process and relevant key points.

Close: End with a powerful image of the message you want the audience to carry away.

must go to great lengths to explain a graphic verbally, then it is not serving your purpose. The graphic should be eliminated or simplified to the point that it clarifies what you have told your audience.

Finally, exercise simplicity and clarity in your use of color, highlighting, and the many other design features included in today's presentation software. Inexperienced presenters often go to excesses in their attempts to develop professional-looking slides and overheads. A real pro, on the other hand, knows that the message comes first. The professional uses fancy design features only to the extent that they serve the message.

For more on the subject of visuals, see appendix C in the back of this book.

Step 6: Rehearse

When would you like to learn about the holes, the dull spots, and the excessive details in your presentation—before or after it's delivered? Naturally, you'd like to find and repair these problems *before-hand*. Identifying weaknesses and honing your delivery are the two purposes of rehearsing.

Consider approaching your presentation as a stage actor would:

1. Learn your lines, fine-tuning them as needed. Pay particular attention to the opening and the closing. These should be particularly solid.

2. Practice delivering your lines—perhaps into a tape recorder.

3. Go back over the rough spots until they're up to par.

4. Wrap it up with a dress rehearsal.

This last point, a dress rehearsal, is especially important if yours is a high-stakes presentation. If you conduct a dress rehearsal, try to do it in the same meeting room or hall where your presentation is scheduled. This will give you a sense of the room, your entryway and exit, and how loud you'll have to be to reach the back row of the audience. If you're lucky, you'll also be able to experiment with the room's sound system and the visual display technology you plan to use.

To make the most of a dress rehearsal, bring along a few objective colleagues. Place some in front, some in the middle, and others in the back row of seats. Then ask them to critique your performance and the effectiveness of the visual aids. Use their comments to bring any weak parts of the presentation up to standard.

Summing Up

This chapter offered a six-step approach to preparing for a speech or presentation.

- **Define your objective.** Here you clarify the outcome you seek. All preparation will serve that objective.

- **Understand the audience.** The better you understand the audience—their familiarity with the subject, how what you have to say will affect them, and so forth—the more you'll be able to craft a presentation that achieves your objective.

- **Decide what to say.** A three-part approach to resolving this important problem was offered: First, define the key message. Second, identify the arguments that support the message. Last, identify where it is important to get audience participation, agreement, or buy-in.

- **Get organized.** This step involves planning what you will say or do in each part of the presentation—the introduction, the narrative, and the other parts.

- **Develop effective visuals.** Many business presentations use visuals to add interest, get information across, and make key points stick with the audience. The chapter offered some tips for creating effective visuals.

- **Rehearse.** Presenters were urged to adopt the rehearsing routine of stage actors: Learn your lines, practice your delivery, go over the rough spots, and use a dress rehearsal.

Show Time

Making an Effective Delivery

Key Topics Covered in This Chapter

- *Speaking effectively*

- *Projecting a positive image*

- *Keeping the audience engaged*

- *Handling questions*

- *Making group presentations*

- *Dealing with stage fright*

- *Evaluating your performance*

ONCE YOU'RE actually in the room with your audience—and you've prepared your message and your materials—you must focus on delivering the most engaging presentation possible. Is this "engaging" part really necessary? you may ask. Isn't content more important than delivery? Not according to Quintilian, an expert on public oration from classical times. As he argued centuries ago, "a mediocre speech supported by all the power of delivery will be more impressive than the best speech unaccompanied by such power."[1]

This chapter offers suggestions on achieving the power of delivery advocated by Quintilian. And, naturally, the first suggestion is about speaking.

Speaking Effectively

Although a course on public speaking lies outside the scope of this book, we can offer some basic suggestions for a good speaking demeanor:

- Do not talk from a script. Talk from your notes only if you have to.

- Avoid jargon and terms unfamiliar to listeners.

- Face your audience, and address different sections in turn.

- Avoid standing behind a podium if you can.

- Walk around your audience, or use movement when you want control, more involvement, or to become one of the group.

- Gesture in a relaxed, natural way—you're not a game-show host.

- Do *not* jingle keys or coins in your pockets.

- Take a deep breath during pauses. It will help you relax and will reduce filler language such as "um" and "er."

In addition to the preceding suggestions, you should use your voice to its best advantage. Enunciate words clearly, keeping your tone natural and conversational, and raising and lowering your voice to make your point. Speak loudly enough for everyone to hear. This is easier to do if you speak to the people in the back rows of the room. Some people find that speaking loudly gives them greater confidence and control. Use a microphone for large groups or a large space, and practice beforehand to find a comfortable speaking volume.

If you're new to public speaking, or if it makes you uncomfortable, take some comfort in knowing that you'll get better at it with repeated experience. Consequently, use every opportunity to get up and present yourself—it's good practice. If you aim to advance to leadership positions throughout your career, effective public speaking is a necessary skill.

Projecting a Positive Image

Image is a factor in effective speaking. In assessing your message, the people in your audience won't rely solely on your words. They will also consider your demeanor and body language. If these do not inspire confidence and commitment, the audience will discount your words. So, to optimize your effectiveness do the following:

- Dress appropriately. You cannot go wrong if dressed as formally or more formally than your audience.

- Make sure your facial expressions convey interest in the audience.

- Rise up to your full posture. This will increase your confidence and give your voice greater volume.

- Make and maintain eye contact with audience members. If you are too nervous to look at the entire audience, focus on individuals instead.

- Avoid "defensive" body language such as folding your arms in front of you.

Keeping the Audience Engaged

Most speakers confront one or several difficult audience members: the tuned out, the overloaded, or people so busy that they are forever thinking about other pressing issues. Neither group will hear what you have to say unless you take measures to break through, grab their attention, and hold onto it.[2]

But how can you tell which members of the audience are attentive and which are not? Psychologists say that people send nonverbal signals about their attentiveness. Those who are following what you say are busy watching you or your visuals, or they are taking notes. Inattentive audience members cross their legs, fidget in their seats, or look around the room more than normal. Your challenge is to attract those wandering minds back to the presentation. Here are some proven techniques for doing so:

- **Change what you're doing.** A sudden pause or change in vocal tone can have the same effect on a preoccupied mind that turning off a television set has on a sleeping viewer: Both these circumstances awaken. Of course, to use this technique successfully, the speaker must follow the pause with something particularly insightful. Otherwise, the inattentive will drift off again.

- **Ask a question.** When you suspect an audience member of taking a mental break, ask a piercing question related to one of your points. "So what does that last point mean for your business?" Suddenly, audience members sense that the ball is in their court. People who weren't listening will probably perk up.

  One award-winning university professor turns the next point in his outline into a question when he senses that his audience is drifting off. To prime them, he'll say, "So now I'm going to ask you a question." He finds that this perks them up.

- **Ask for a show of hands.** Passivity ensures that some minds will wander. You can eliminate passivity by engaging people in your argument, as in these examples: "Just out of curiosity, how many of you believe that your customers are satisfied with our current returns policy? Let's see a show of hands." "I've just suggested two allocation alternatives for this client's portfolio. Can anyone suggest a third? Emma, do you have one in mind?"

- **Put your audience in the hot seat.** Remember how some of your teachers randomly picked students to go to the board and work out math problems? You had to pay attention because you might be the next one picked. A similar technique can be used in maintaining audience attention: "I'm going to spend the next few minutes describing our client's problem and how we're currently approaching it. Then I'd like some thoughts from you on alternative approaches."

- **Add humor.** Many writers, especially playwrights, use humor to good effect. They inject it strategically into long pieces of serious drama to create contrast and to provide relief for the audience—hence the term *comic relief.* You can achieve the same effect in a serious business presentation.

  Humor is most effective when used with large audiences and when used sparingly. It is less useful in small settings because speakers command attention by the power of their presence, a power that diminishes as the audience grows larger and more physically detached from the speaker.

- **Use visuals to good effect** Visuals can augment your verbal delivery and keep your audience alert and engaged (see chapter 7). A bold visual has a magnetic effect on an audience.

  Visuals have the opposite effect, however, when speakers rely on them to tell the whole story—particularly when they simply read what the audience is capable of reading for itself. Have you ever heard a presenter say, "OK, what this slide is saying is . . . "? That phrase will be repeated to deadening effect throughout the talk, indicating that the speaker hasn't thought about the connections between the slides and the main thrust of the presentation. Don't make this mistake.

Handling Questions

Questions taken from the audience can both engage the listeners and provide you with opportunities to furnish greater detail in areas that matter to listeners. The best time for "Q&A" is at the very end; this allows you to complete your delivery as planned. It's also a good idea to let the audience know at the very beginning that you'll provide time for questions at the end. Doing so has two benefits: It prevents unwanted interruptions, and it ensures that listeners will have heard your entire presentation *before* they ask questions. Taking questions during the presentation keeps people engaged and gives you feedback about how well they understand your message. But this approach may cause you to lose control of your talk.

Anticipate Likely Questions

Q&A entails risk for the presenter. If he or she must repeatedly say, "I don't know," "I'm not sure," or "I'll have to get back to you on that," the credibility of the presentation will suffer. That risk can be reduced if the speaker anticipates and develops answers for likely questions as part of the presentation preparation.

You can anticipate likely questions if you take the trouble to

Case Study: Under Fire with Questions

You're a senior manager responsible for developing a new software product that is late to market and far over budget. You've been asked to rally the troops and urge them on. You finish your talk with some stirring words about pioneers and landing on the moon. You hope that your remarks didn't sound too goofy, and then it's time for Q&A. The first question comes from a guy in the back.

"Pardon my skepticism, but we've been hearing this same stuff from senior management for months now. We don't need another pep talk. What we really need is more help and a lot less red tape."

It's the question you most feared. You begin to think that your speech has had no impact. You take a deep breath, and respond.

"The fact is that we're committed to getting you more help. We're struggling to hire qualified people. But as you know, qualified software developers are very hard to find right now. And we don't want to create more problems by hiring second-best personnel who will make your work more difficult. If you know qualified software developers, please tell us who they are.

"As for red tape, we'd like to think that we eliminated most of it when we set you up in a separate building and organized the project into self-managing teams. Next question?"

understand your audience. Who will come to the presentation? Why are they coming? What are their concerns? How is the presentation likely to strike them? For example, if your presentation concerns the adoption of a new employee dental insurance plan, you'll want to have answers to specific and predictable questions at the ready—unless you cover them in the body of the presentation:

How much will employees have to contribute to the plan each month?

Is there an annual deductible that employees must pay before the plan benefits kick in?

Does the plan cover orthodontia?

Are all family members automatically covered by the plan?

If not, what is the cost of additional coverage?

It's impossible to anticipate and prepare for every question that may come your way. For this reason, you must be prepared to think on your feet and know how to redirect questions. In this respect, you have four tools: feedback, paraphrasing, clarification, and empathy.[3]

Give Feedback

Feedback is a form of two-way communication. A person says something, and you respond, giving your reaction to what was said, as in the accompanying example.

On the surface, in this example, you've responded to each of the points raised by the questioner. And yet, your response may do little to cure the questioner's negative attitude—an attitude that others may share. You could have done more, as demonstrated next.

Paraphrase the Question

Paraphrasing the question is a technique for mirroring the questioner's points. It indicates that you are listening and interested in what that person has to say. Let's look at how this tool works in the same example.

So what you're saying is that I'm just giving the party line when what you really need is more help and less red tape, is that right?

The questioner's likely response is yes. Now the hostile questioner is agreeing with you. You can then go on to give your feedback, in the words used in the case study example, but to a more receptive listener. But there are even better ways to respond.

Clarify the Issues

In clarifying the issues, you work a little harder with the questioner's words to identify his or her real concerns. Let's see how that would happen here.

> *So, what I hear you saying is that you see two key problems: too few people and too much red tape. The first is probably the most important. Is that right?*

Again, you've established a level of agreement with the questioner. By clarifying, however, you've gone a step further. You've shown the audience that you can think on your feet and that you're genuinely interested in trying to sort out the vital issues. In this way, you keep better control of the Q&A session.

Demonstrate Empathy

Empathy is the ability to identify with or vicariously experience the thoughts or feelings of others. Anything you can do during a presentation to demonstrate genuine empathy will improve your standing with the audience and help neutralize any subliminal hostility. As President Bill Clinton was so fond of stating, "I feel your pain." Members of the audience who sense genuine empathy will think, "She understands our problems," or "She's really one of us. We can trust her."

The Q&A session is one of the obvious places where you can demonstrate empathy with your audience, as in our software project example.

> *I recognize the hardship that long hours and too few helping hands have caused people on your team. One person told me just last week about how she had to miss her daughter's first soccer game. I have young kids, too, so I know how she must feel. That's why we're sending HR people to every software job fair and pulling out all the stops in finding qualified people to lighten your load.*

Tips for Handling Q&A

The following tips can help you and your listeners get the full benefit from your presentation.

- Make a clear transition to the Q&A session.

- If the audience is large, repeat the question for the audience to hear.

- Maintain control of Q&A by rephrasing the question and giving the answer to the whole group, not only to the questioner.

- If you don't know the answer to a question, direct the person to a source for the answer, or offer to get the answer later.

- If you get a hostile question, find out the reasons for the hostility. Acknowledge valid points, and reject those that are not accurate. Then politely move on.

- Don't allow a long-winded questioner to monopolize the Q&A session. Say, "So that other people get a chance to talk, let me stop you there and see if I can answer the question."

Making Group Presentations

In some cases, you will want other people to contribute to your presentation. For example, you may be presenting the results of a group effort, or you may want your collaborators to help you achieve your communication objective.

Group presentations should divide up the speakers either by credibility with the audience, their presentation skills, or their known expertise in particular areas. For example, a team making a case for a new product line might select its most credible and articulate member to handle the opening and closing—where persuasiveness matters the most. Once the presentation shifts to marketing issues, a person with widely acknowledged marketing skills should lead that part.

A typical group presentation flows as follows: The first speaker introduces the other speakers briefly and introduces the topic. Each subsequent speaker provides a transition to the next one with a sentence: "Now, June will cover . . ." The final speaker provides the closing.

Visuals pose challenges for a group presentation. Unmanaged, each speaker could end up with a different medium and no continuity with the rest of the speaking team. This lack of coordination could create a hodgepodge appearance and lots of unprofessional fumbling around with equipment. Extra planning and coordination can prevent this. One approach is to assign the organization of visuals to one team member. He or she would make sure that all slides or overheads adopt the same format, that they use the same projection equipment, and so forth.

The Q&A session is another area of concern for group presenters. You want to avoid a situation in which someone asks a question and three people start to answer at the same time—or worse, everyone is closed-mouthed and looking back and forth as if to say, "Should I take this, or will you?" Plan in advance how the group will handle questions, and you'll avoid this type of fumbling. Generally, each speaker should be prepared to answer questions in his or her particular area and to follow up if other team members need help. By all means, *do not* have every speaker comment about every question.

Dealing with Stage Fright

Do your anxiety levels go up whenever your turn at the speaker's podium draws near? Does nervousness cause you to fumble as you begin to speak? If you said yes to either of these questions, you're in good company. Even professional speakers and stage actors get the jitters. Acclaimed actor Ian Holm had such a case of stage fright early in his career that he switched to movie acting and didn't return to live audiences for decades.

Fortunately, you can be a successful presenter even if you never get rid of the jitters entirely. The key is learning to handle your fear.

Handling your fear begins early on, when you're developing the presentation. Pack your presentation with ideas and facts about which you are enthusiastic and fully confident, and you'll be less nervous. If anything seems dubious—making you swallow hard before saying it—then take it out. Enthusiasm and confidence in your material will help calm your nerves.

Then, once your presentation is solid, rehearse it until you can deliver it with minimal notes. And since many people are most unnerved and wobbly when they first being talking, put extra work into the opening. A smooth, confident opening will put you into a winning frame of mind for the rest of your speech.

Here are a few more suggestions for handling fear:

- Anticipate questions and objections, and develop solid responses.

- Understand your audience. Speaking before an assembly of people whom you understand is always less nerve-wracking than addressing a group of strangers. You may even want to meet audience members individually by telephone before the presentation, or in person as they come into the room.

- Use breathing techniques and tension-relieving exercises to reduce stress.

- Stop thinking about yourself and how you appear to the audience. Switch your thoughts to the audience and how your presentation can help them.

- Accept nervousness as natural, and do not try to counteract it with food, caffeine, drugs, or alcohol prior to the presentation.

- If all else fails and you start getting the shakes, pick out a friendly face in the audience and talk to that person.

Evaluating Your Presentation

Like other activities, a speech or presentation is the result of a process that converts inputs (your ideas, information, and arguments) to outputs (what your audience sees and hears). And like other processes, it can be improved.

Process improvement—whether it has to do with making automobiles or presentations to the board of directors—is the foundation of quality. The quality movement that swept through manufacturing in the 1980s and through services in succeeding years has taught us that if we want a higher level of output quality, we should look first to the output itself. Is it up to standard, or are there measurable defects? When defects are found, we must trace them back to the process that produced them. In most cases, this will pinpoint the root cause of the defect. Once the root cause is known, we can take corrective action.

Follow this same approach after every presentation. A presentation is not an automobile or another manufactured good. But if you take the time to objectively evaluate a presentation after the fact (or after a rehearsal), you will be able to pinpoint the root causes of poor performance. For example, you may find cluttered overheads, weak opening remarks, inept attempts at humor, or something else. Once you've identified the problems, do something about them as you prepare for your next presentation.

One of the best ways to evaluate your performance and to pinpoint areas for improvement is to videotape each presentation (or rehearsal) for later review. If this is not possible, ask one or more helpful colleagues to take note of what went well and what went poorly. An after-action review of the tape or the colleagues' notes will put you in touch with the best and worst of your presentation skills. If you work on continuous improvement, your presentations will become more and more effective—and your standing in the organization will rise.

Summing Up

This chapter discussed the effective delivery, that is, where attention to principles and preparation will pay off. The chapter addressed how to get your ideas across and make an impact on the audience. It also considered the unique requirements of group presentations, the problem of stage fright, and the importance of performance evaluation.

- Effective speaking is the first and most obvious requirement of effective delivery. Various tips were given on this important activity.

- Projecting a positive image is equally important. You want the audience to take you seriously.

- Keeping the audience engaged is another requirement. You can engage your listeners by periodically changing what you are doing, asking questions, injecting humor, and using appealing visuals.

- Question and answer sessions are a feature of many presentations. You will be more effective in the Q&A part of your presentation if you anticipate likely questions, provide feedback, and demonstrate empathy for the audience.

- Group presentations present a few organizational issues. The foremost of these is the question of who talks when. Speaking chores should be assigned by either the speaker's credibility with the audience, individual presentation skills, or recognized expertise in different areas.

- Stage fright is a regular companion of most public speakers. Although it may never be completely conquered, stage fright can be controlled through solid preparation, knowledge of the audience, and other tips offered in this chapter.

- The evaluation of a presentation is the last step of effective delivery. Creating and delivering a presentation is a process that, like every other process, can be improved. To do so, you need to step back and evaluate what went well and what went badly. Once you identify the root causes of below-par performance, you can address them.

Dialogue

The Ultimate Communication

Key Topics Covered in This Chapter

- *Understanding the other person*

- *Seeing yourself (or your company) from the other person's perspective*

- *Creating dialogue*

EVERYTHING you've read about business communication to this point has been about writing and making presentations or speeches. These two forms of communication are extremely important in the business world, and improving each will help you in your career. But the truth is that most workplace communication takes place between two people. Examples include a formal performance evaluation session between a manager and a subordinate, an informal meeting in which a boss tries to mentor a promising employee, a telephone conversation between a supplier and a customer, the banter between two colleagues on a flight to their annual sales conference, a lunch meeting. The list goes on.

Though we don't always recognize it, each of these moments involves business communication. More important, each provides an opportunity to pursue the purposes of business communication: to advance our agendas, to share information with others, and to build relationships—opportunities that should never be wasted.

This chapter examines three principles for effective one-on-one communications: understanding the other person, seeing your point of view from the other person's perspective, and creating dialogue. Master these, and many of your communication problems will take care of themselves.

Case Study: Don't Forget Your Homework!

Carla, director of strategic planning, thought that she was well prepared for her meeting with Shirley, director of the company's newsletter unit. Carla's goal was twofold: to explain plans to form a joint venture with a weekly business magazine and to win Shirley's support. She assumed that Shirley would share her enthusiasm for that venture.

Shirley's icy demeanor should have been a signal that the plan did not sit well with her, but, being wrapped up in her own enthusiasm for the plan, Carla failed to detect the signal as she explained the goal of the joint venture and its details. "So you can see why we're all very excited about this venture," Carla concluded, "and the opportunity to get broader distribution for some of the newsletter pieces your people put together."

Shirley paused for a moment and then spoke in a measured tone. "As you know, Carla, our newsletter subscriptions have grown by at least 20 percent per year during each of the past three years. We are doing very, very well." She leaned forward slightly as she continued. "And the reason for our success is that we have focused on the specific interests of our subscriber base. Are you proposing that we jeopardize that success by shifting gears and writing for a general audience?"

Carla did not have a satisfactory answer for Shirley, because she hadn't anticipated her negative attitude toward the joint venture. And so her attempt at communication failed. Worse, she had antagonized an important member of management.

Understanding the Other Person

Most material on writing and presentations begins with this piece of advice: Know your audience. This advice applies equally to one-on-one communication.

Who is the person sitting across the table from you?

How much does he or she know about the issue that you plan to discuss?

Does the person have a point of view on that issue? What is it?

How will his or her work be affected by what you have to say?

These are the types of questions you should try to answer before opening your mouth.

You can reduce the chance of the type of failure that Carla experienced by doing two things: First, do your homework. Learn what you can about the other person and how he or she will be affected by what you have to say. Second, anticipate problems. If you understand the other person, you are more likely to think of his or her objections to what you plan to say. Once you've identified likely objections, you can prepare yourself with satisfactory responses.

Seeing Yourself (or Your Company) from the Other Person's Perspective

"O would some power the gift to give us, to see ourselves as others see us." Robert Burns got it right a long time ago: Part of understanding the party with whom you're communicating is understanding how that person perceives you—and your company if the person is a nonemployee. Does he or she view you favorably, perhaps as someone with good ideas or as someone who is reliable and truthful? Does the person view you negatively because of some past conflict? Or would the word *neutral* best describe the person's perception of you? Failing to understand how you are perceived can undermine your effort to communicate.

Like Jon, you can improve your one-on-one communication by determining how you or your company is perceived by the other party. Armed with that knowledge, you'll be in a better position to get what you want from every encounter.

Case Study: But What Do They Think of Us?

Jon, a senior vice president of Globetrot Consulting, was assigned the task of meeting and possibly recruiting Phil, a successful consultant working for a competing firm. Jon had heard from a former client that Phil wasn't happy with his current situation and that he was looking for something new. Since Phil was well thought of in corporate circles, Jon called him and the two arranged to meet for lunch the next week.

Jon learned as much as he could about Phil in the days before their meeting. He learned that Phil had earned an M.B.A. in 1988 from Old Ivy, a first-tier school; had joined a Fortune 500 company as a strategic planner upon graduation; and had worked for two major consulting firms in strategy since then. Jon had also exploited his corporate network to gather insights from Phil's former clients. All in all, Jon managed to learn quite a bit about this prospective recruit.

What Jon didn't know was what Phil thought about Globetrot Consulting. Had their paths ever crossed? Had Globetrot interviewed Phil during his final year as an M.B.A. student back in 1988, or again when he switched from industry to consulting? Had Globetrot ever offered employment to Phil? Jon called his human resource department to get the answers.

While he waited, Jon turned to other sources. Since management consulting is a small, almost inbred profession, he figured that someone in the firm must know Phil. He therefore put out a confidential inquiry within the firm: "Who knows this guy?" He also checked with the many firm members who were alumni of Old Ivy's M.B.A. program.

Within a few days, he had responses from the human resource department and from three Globetrot employees who personally knew Phil. Human Resources reported interesting news. The firm had made a job offer to Phil back in 1988, when he graduated from Old Ivy, but he had turned it down to go

Continued

into industry. Globetrot had made him another offer in 1992, when he first went into consulting, with the same negative result.

This was interesting information. Did Phil have a negative view of the firm? What was the issue? Jon's phone calls to colleagues who knew Phil answered these questions. "Yes, I know Phil fairly well," said a former Old Ivy classmate. "He's never taken our firm seriously, because he thinks that we're not fully competitive in strategic planning." Other contacts related much the same story.

Jon was now much better prepared for his one-on-one meeting with Phil. He knew Phil's background *and* Phil's perception of Globetrot Consulting. When the two met the next week, Jon was totally prepared to talk about Globetrot's growing strength in strategic planning and how Phil could play a leadership role.

Creating Dialogue

Everything we've said about communication prior to this chapter involved a one-way flow of written or spoken words. In this arrangement, the writer or presenter is like a radio or TV station, transmitting a message while offering the audience no direct opportunity to immediately respond. Sure, e-mail allows a message receiver to send a reply very quickly, and presentations are generally followed by Q&A sessions in which the audience has a chance to talk back. These, however, are serial conversations, which are not the same as genuine two-way communication, in which one person makes a statement and the other person follows immediately with a response. And two-way communication—or dialogue—is usually the very best way to peel back the layers of problems, develop solutions, and reach common understandings. One-way communication is fine for sharing information, but dialogue is essential when you need a meeting of the minds.

Though the practice of dialogue between two or more individuals undoubtedly goes back into the mists of time, Plato, through his Socratic dialogues, helped the Western world appreciate the power of dialogue as a mode of communication. Plato's purpose was not to tell us what *he* or Socrates thought, but to teach us how to toss ideas back and forth in a logical process that eventually leads to the truth. It is that same logical, back-and-forth process that produces better business decisions and resolves differences between individuals.

As an effective communicator—and as a leader—you should encourage dialogue on the critical and complex issues facing the organization. This is usually the best way to draw out the best ideas and build agreement around them. Dialogue can also help you give direction without telling people what to do in so many words—an important practice in workplaces that rely on participatory management. For example, instead of saying, "Have the inventory report on my desk at three P.M. tomorrow," try something like this:

Manager: *What progress have you made on the inventory report?*

Employee: *It's almost ready. I only have one section to complete.*

Manager: *Good. Do you see any problem with getting it all wrapped up by tomorrow afternoon?*

Employee: *No, not if you need it by then.*

Manager: *Yes, I need it by three P.M. tomorrow at the latest.*

Employee: *You can count on it.*

Notice how much was disclosed in this dialogue that would not have been disclosed in the simple directive "Have the inventory report on my desk at three P.M. tomorrow."

1. The manager learned the state of progress on the report: "I only have one section to complete."

2. The employee was given an opportunity to report any barriers to progress: "Do you see any problem with getting it all wrapped up by tomorrow afternoon?"

Catchball as Dialogue

Among their other contributions to management methods, the Japanese have given us *catchball*. Catchball is a cross-functional method for accomplishing two things: idea enrichment/improvement, and buy-in among participants.

Here's how it works. An initial idea is "tossed" to the organization for consideration. The idea may be a new strategic goal, a new product, or a way to improve some work process. Whoever "catches" the idea assumes responsibility for understanding it, reflecting on it, and improving it in some way. That person then tosses the improved idea back to the group, where it is again caught and improved. And around it goes in a cycle of gradual improvement. As people participate, they develop a sense of shared ownership and commitment to the idea that takes form (figure 9-1).

Catchball may have "Made in Japan" written all over it, but its underlying principle goes back to the Socratic method of dialogue described to us by Plato. The next time your organization needs to develop a raw idea and get people committed to it, try catchball.[1]

3. The manager shared his own time constraint with the employee: "I need it by three P.M. tomorrow at the latest."

4. The employee made an informal contract with the manager: "You can count on it."

Dialogue is thus a much richer exchange of information and helps create a bond of trust and commitment between the two parties.

Active Listening

Effective dialogue requires what some call *active listening*. At a minimum, active listening means giving the other person your respect-

FIGURE 9-1

Catchball Figure

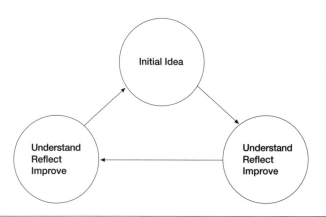

ful and undivided attention. Beyond absorbing what that person is saying, active listening implies attention to the emotions behind the spoken words. These emotions are generally signaled through body language and the speaker's vocal delivery.

Are You Hearing the Truth?

Dialogue is only as effective as the verbal inputs of participants. In a perfect world, everyone speaks the truth. But we don't live in a perfect world—especially when we're at work. People have strong incentives to conceal facts, hedge the truth, and even lie. This creates a problem for effective dialogue.

How can we know when we're not getting a straight story? In some cases, untruths are self-revealing: A person's story simply doesn't add up, or what you're hearing conflicts with other information. But some untruths are not self-revealing. Is it possible to know when someone is telling you a lie?

According to Paul Ekman, who has studied and written on this problem, spotting a liar is hard, because most of the standard clues we have come to associate with liars and lying don't offer much help. Shifty eyes, for example, may only indicate nervousness or shy-

Tips for Active Listening

You'll be a more active listener if you adopt the following practices when you interact with other people.

- Lean toward the speaker to signal your attention.

- Maintain eye contact.

- Smile. It will put the other person at ease.

- Avoid anything that will distract your attention; take notes only if necessary.

- Be sensitive to your body language, such as posture and arm position.

- Listen first and evaluate later.

- Don't interrupt the other person except to ask questions for clarification.

- Encourage the other person to continue by repeating in your own words what you think was said.

- Formulate your response only *after* the other person has finished speaking.

ness. A liar who has convinced himself or herself that the falsehoods are true can tell a raging lie while looking us straight in the eyes. Our own wish to believe what the person is telling us can also make a lie difficult to detect.

For those who want to separate truth from fiction, Ekman offers a few tips:

- **Slips of the tongue:** For example, someone says, "I don't love that idea—I mean, I *do* love that idea." This slip could indicate a lie.

- **An erratic gesture or a change in voice timbre:** Nervousness or guilt may cause these anomalies.

- **An abnormal amount of hand waving as the person speaks:** This may reveal a concealed emotion.

- **"Micro–expressions" on the face:** Look for a fleeting frown that betrays the smile, or a brief expression of disgust.[2]

Ekman's tips might help you catch an occasion fib as you conduct dialogue with fellow workers and others, but you'll never catch all the falsehoods. In the long run, the best antidote to untruthful communication is an organization climate that expects straight talking and does not tolerate liars.

Summing Up

Most communication that takes place in the workplace isn't written or delivered through stand-up speeches or presentations. It's one-on-one. This chapter presented three ways in which you can make those one-on-one exchanges more effective and productive.

- **Understanding the other person:** Our know-the-audience principle applies equally to one-on-one communications. Consequently, try to understand the perspective of the person, what he or she already knows, the person's point of view, and how he or she will be affected by what you have to say.

- **Seeing yourself (or your company) from the other person's perspective:** You'll be a more effective communicator if you can get inside the other person's head and see how you or your company appears from that vantage point.

- **Creating dialogue:** Dialogue is qualitatively different from the one-way communication that characterizes business writing and most other presentations. Dialogue allows two or more parties to bounce ideas back and forth and, in the process, reveals more information and helps people converge on solutions.

Useful Implementation Tools

This appendix contains four forms that you may find useful when planning an oral presentation or a written document. Forms one and two are adapted from Harvard ManageMentor, an online help source for subscribers. Forms three and four are adapted from *The Instant-Answer Guide to Business Writing* by Deborah Dumaine and the Better Communications® Team. For all four interactive versions of these worksheets, please visit www.elearning.hbsp.org/businesstools.

1. **Preliminary planning worksheet:** Use this worksheet to help you plan the content of your presentation.

2. **Presentation outline worksheet:** Once you have planned what you want to say, use this worksheet to help you organize your content most effectively, to identify any visual aids or support materials that will enhance your presentation, and to estimate the time you will need. You may have to revise your content if it appears to exceed your time limitations.

3. **"Be your own editor" checklist:** This worksheet offers guidance for editing. Before releasing a document, verify for yourself that you have considered each item.

4. **Design for visual impact:** Use this guide for a quick reminder of how to design your document for easy reading.

Preliminary Planning Worksheet

Use this worksheet to help you plan the content of your presentation.

Topic:
Requested by:

Objectives

If your presentation is a success, what will be the immediate results?

Main Messages

What must the audience understand and remember from your presentation?

1.

2.

3.

4.

5.

Supporting Facts

What facts support your main message?

Message 1

Message 2

Message 3

Message 4

Message 5

Source: HMM Making a Presentation.

Presentation Outline Worksheet

Once you have planned what you want to say, use this worksheet to help you organize your content most effectively, identify any visual aids or support materials that will enhance your presentation, and estimate the time you will need. You may have to revise your content if it appears to exceed your time limitations.

Your Content	Visuals/Support Materials	Time
Opening • State your purpose. • Preview your main points. • Make your audience want to listen.		
Body • Get across the main points of your presentation.		
Conclusion • Summarize your content. • Challenge the audience to take action.		

Source: HMM Making a Presentation.

FIGURE A-3

"Be Your Own Editor" Checklist

The questions below reflect easy-to-overlook aspects of editing. Before releasing a document, verify for yourself that you have considered each item.

Content

Purpose: ☐ Stated clearly?   ☐ Specific requests for action or information?

Information: ☐ Accurate and complete?   ☐ Right amount of detail?

Sequence

Bottom Line: ☐ At the top?   ☐ Strategically placed?

Organization: ☐ Ideas flow logically?

Design

Format: ☐ Enough headlines, sidelines, and lists?   ☐ Deadlines and action items highlighted?
    ☐ White space to frame ideas?

Presentation: ☐ Would a chart, table, or graph be more effective for certain information?

Structure

Paragraphs: ☐ Begin with a topic sentence?   ☐ Transitions within and between?
    ☐ Focused on one topic?   ☐ Limited to 5 to 6 lines?

Sentences: ☐ Varied in structure and length?   ☐ Streamlined to 15 to 20 words?

Tone/Style

Words: ☐ Simple, specific, and straightforward? ☐ Terminology familiar to readers?
    ☐ Free of affectation and stuffy outdated language?   ☐ Headlines designed for impact?
    ☐ Acronyms explained?

Style: ☐ Personable, upbeat, and direct?   ☐ Active voice?
    ☐ Appropriate for the audience?   ☐ Positive approach?

Proofread

    ☐ Grammar, spelling, and punctuation accurate?   ☐ Should someone else review this?
    ☐ Typographical errors corrected?   ☐ If this is a repeat mailing, is new data highlighted?

Other   *Enter your own editorial "trouble spots" to double-check and prevent.*

Source: HMM Writing for Business.

Design for Visual Impact

Use this guide as a quick reminder of how to design your document for easy reading.

You Can Use . . .	To . . .
Headlines	• introduce most paragraphs • focus your reader on your major ideas
Sidelines	• add extra emphasis • aid in persuasion
Text fonts	• assure readability • unify style
Short paragraphs	• avoid overwhelming your reader • attract speed readers
Two columns	• convey two kinds of information simultaneously • encourage faster reading
Bulleted lists	• replace lists within sentences
Numbered lists	• indicate sequence • list steps in a procedure • provide easy reference to the list • quantify items
White space and indentation	• frame your ideas • improve readability
Graphs, charts, and tables	• present numbers, dollar amounts, and technical data
Color (use judiciously)	• highlight information (limit to two colors) • add aesthetic appeal
underlining **bold typeface** different fonts ALL CAPITALS *italics* different type sizes	• emphasize deadlines and action items

Source: HMM Writing for Business.

Writing the Perfect Job Application Cover Letter

Business writer Michael E. Hattersley shared his thoughts on writing cover letters in the *Harvard Management Communication Letter*.[1] Since job applications can be so crucial to a person's career, we reprint this article for our readers.

It's a throwaway, right? The letter you attach to your résumé saying you want that job interview. The résumé will do the heavy lifting. The cover letter is just there because—well, because you need a cover letter.

But in business, every single piece of communication matters. Picture the average boss hunting for a new employee. She's got a pile of applications. She will go through the stack and rapidly narrow the candidates down to a few who fit the profile she's looking for.

Let's say half a dozen candidates survive, and the boss has time to interview three people. This is the point at which the cover letter becomes crucial. If it's done right, it can get you that interview.

Here are a few rules of thumb for winning cover letters:

1. **Open avenues of conversation.** Before writing your cover letter, get one of the standard guides on how to do a good job interview. Emphasize aspects of your background that play into typical most-asked questions.

2. **Make the hirer want to find out more about you.** Don't be so exhaustive in your cover letter that there's nothing left to dis-

cuss in an interview. Except in very special circumstances, your
letter should fit on a page. Often half a page is enough.

3. **Show you're familiar with the organization you're applying to.**
   If you don't know the company, spend an hour in the library
   reading its latest annual report or search the Internet for information.

4. **Emphasize how your education and training especially qualify
   you.** For example, suggest tactfully that you're overqualified
   for your current position and it's time to move on.

5. **Be crisp and punchy.** By the time the boss gets to your letter,
   he may have read a hundred résumés. You want to grab attention while still maintaining a sense of style. Convey an ener-
   getic image through forceful writing. Use active rather than
   passive or intransitive verbs. Don't ramble. Make sure each
   paragraph has a clear thesis sentence and conveys a complete
   unit of thought.

6. **Don't make any mistakes.** Good writing matters; it can
   demonstrate to a prospective employer how well you can
   manage information. Proof carefully, and run the letter by a
   friend or colleague for suggestions.

7. **Make use of personal contacts.** If you know people who may
   have influence on the hiring decision, let them know you're
   interested either by personal contact or by copying them on
   the cover letter.

Create an Argument That Fits the Purpose

Once past these general rules, however, the design of your cover letter depends on the type of job search. Are you highly qualified for
the job, or are you taking a long shot? Is the organization seeking
someone like you, or will you be appearing out of the blue?
Consider the following guidelines:

If you're highly qualified for the job, argue from experience: "I've had a terrific record as an assistant product manager at Company X, and I now feel ready to become product manager at Company Y." Highlight the experiences and any specific successes you have had that make you just right for the job.

If, as in most cases, you have the right general background for the job but haven't been doing exactly the same thing at a lower level, argue from skills and analogy: "The training I've received as a production line manager gives me the background I need to become a quality control inspector." Show how your skills are clearly transferable to the new job.

If you're not qualified for the job and you're not the type of person the organization would normally recruit, your only choice is to argue from interest: "Although I currently work on an oil rig, I've always wanted to be a fashion designer." It may sound absurd, but this approach works more often than you might expect. If you do have transferable skills, point them out.

Use a Structure That Fits the Argument

Good conventional cover letters adopt a Me-You-We model. Structure your letter using the standard logical formula established by Socrates: Given-Since-Therefore:

- **Me (first paragraph):** I'm very interested in this job, and I have the following qualifications for it.

- **You (second paragraph):** The following aspects of your organization challenge me and ensure I can make a contribution to it.

- **We (third paragraph):** We will work well together, and you should give me the job.

There's at least one exception to the Me-You-We structure, however: the broadcast letter. This is a case where you're casting a very wide net with the hope that you'll snag at least one or two expressions of interest. Say you're writing to every consulting firm listed in the library because you have a narrow but deep area of expertise. In this case, you have nothing to lose by being bold. In effect, you're trying to create a job opportunity, not applying for an existing position. Here you need to grab the reader's attention in a very short space. List your accomplishments vividly: "I've doubled my department's sales in two years" or "My job at Company X has allowed me to gain more knowledge of Y than anyone else in the country." Then close with a quick query about whether they might have a position that fits your background.

But Enough About "I"

Avoid the worst fault of most cover letters, the "I" phenomenon. Overuse of "I" can make you sound grandiose or self-obsessed when you actually want to portray yourself as a team player. It's hard to sell yourself without using the word "I" a lot, but there are several alternatives to starting every sentence with it. Sometimes you can bury the "I" within the sentence: instead of "I was the best performer in the computer services department," try "While working in the computer services department, I accomplished A and B and received the top ratings from my superiors among twenty colleagues." Don't have "I's" lead every paragraph, where they take on undue prominence and leap off the page. Even "my" or "me" makes a softer substitute.

Cover letters may be tossed aside, but often they're one of the last things the hirer will review before interviewing you. It's crucial that your writing makes a strong case to the prospective employer for their taking the next step with your application.

Commonsense Rules for Presentation Visuals

Software programs such as Microsoft's PowerPoint, Corel Presentations, Harvard Graphics, and others have made it possible for businesspeople to enhance their presentations with eye-catching text, charts, and graphs. The programs offer immense color and design features: three-dimensional effects, many font choices, clip art, and much more. When used judiciously, these programs can create visuals that convey more information in less time than would more traditionally prepared visual aids. High-tech visuals can get key points across and make them memorable. In the wrong hands, however, these powerful tools can actually confuse or bore the audience, diminishing the impact of an entire presentation. Here are a few rules for making the most of presentation visuals.

Rule 1: Subordinate Your Visuals to Your Message

You and what you have to say should always be the focus of the presentation. Visuals should therefore play no more than a supportive role. They should never command center stage. Presenters can observe this important rule by following these guidelines:

- Don't try to say everything through overheads.

- Refrain from simply reading your overheads to the audience.

- Avoid visuals that are not essential to the presentation.

Rule 2: Keep Your Visuals Simple

Some presenters clutter every overhead with border-to-border text, as in example A. Extra words detract from the presenter's message and make the audience work unnecessarily hard to capture key points.

Example A is overburdened with text. It contains information better conveyed verbally by the speaker. Example B, in contrast, captures the key points without the supporting details. These points are clear and easy to remember.

Example A [Cluttered]: Challenges for the Coming Year

The sales force must become more efficient next year. Currently, selling costs are running close to 20 percent of revenues. The industry average is 14 percent.

On average, we have fifteen days of finished goods inventory. Financing and maintaining that inventory is expensive. If we were better at forecasting sales, we could cut that inventory level—perhaps by as much as four days. That would save the company close to $50,000 per year.

Our workforce needs more training to stay competitive. We should aim for forty hours of training for all nonprofessional employees and sixty hours for professional employees.

Example B [Simple]: Challenges for the Coming Year

- Greater sales efficiency
- Less finished goods inventory
- More training for everyone

Rule 3: Use a Minimum of Devices

People who take the time to master presentation software are tempted to use many of their "cool" devices: different colors, many font styles and sizes, shading, and on and on. Don't fall into this trap. Those devices can deflect attention from the message. Ask yourself, "Do I need the fancy fill effects and the clip art? Would one font style be better than the three I'm using?" In most cases, your visuals will look more professional if you use a bare minimum of devices. Simpler is usually better.

Rule 4: Make Your Images Large and Legible

Your visuals should be clearly legible to everyone in the room—even those in the back row of seats. If you've observed rules 2 and 3, then you'll have plenty of room on each slide or overhead to make your images large.

Rule 5: Use Graphics to Tell Key Parts of the Story

Most people are visually oriented. They perceive and digest information best when it's presented graphically.

For example, a speaker wants to make the point that one product model has outsold two others. He could simply tell his audience, "Results for the previous twelve months indicate that model C outsold both models A and B." He could also put this information in an overhead containing the following sentence: "Model C has outsold both model A and model B during the past twelve months."

The speaker could then go on to detail the relative sales of these three models. Alternatively, he could use a graphic image that shows the relative sales performance of the three models in unit numbers (figure C-1).

FIGURE C-1

12-Month Sales Models A, B, C

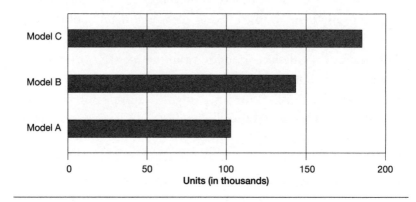

To show your audience the greatest impact, reserve graphics like those in figure C-1 for the key points of your presentation. If you create visuals for everything, the key points will be lost in the clutter.

Rule 6: Use the Most Appropriate Graphic Form

Most presentation programs and their spreadsheet supporting systems allow you to produce pie charts, column charts, bar charts, line charts, column charts, scattergrams, and so forth. Each is best for presenting certain types of data. Figure C-1 illustrates a bar chart and how it can be used. There are other forms of graphics that you can also consider.

Pie Charts

Pie charts are best when your goal is to show the impact of different factors on the whole. Thus, if you wanted your audience to understand the contributions of your company's three product models to total sales revenue, a pie chart would be your best choice (figure C-2). Each is shown as a slice of the entire pie.

FIGURE C - 2

12-Month Sales Models A, B, C

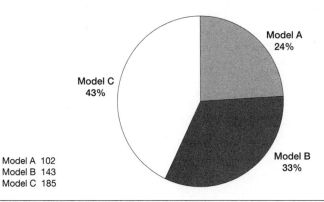

Bar and Column Charts

Use bar and column charts when you want the audience to compare outcomes, such as in the model A, B, C bar chart shown earlier in figure C-1. In that chart, the audience could see *both* the relative performances of the three different models and their actual
unit sales. That's something they won't see in a pie chart.

Line Charts

Line charts are particularly good at indicating trends. In figure C-3,
we show the change in the share price of XYZ Corporation over
time—January through December 2002. If we were comparing its
price trend to that of a competitor, we could easily put them on the
same chart.

Scattergrams

If you want to show a statistical linear regression (the best fit of a
line drawn through a number of scattered data points), exponential
smoothing, or a moving average, a scattergram is your best bet.
These types of charts are invaluable when you have many data

FIGURE C-3

**Average Monthly Stock Price
XYZ Corporation**

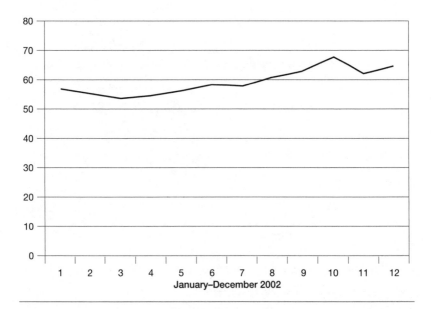

points for one specific variable, for example, the sales revenues from fifty branch stores for each month of a year. Figure C-4 maps data points along the *x* (time) and *y* (returns) axes. In the figure, we created a best-fit trend line based on statistical linear regression for a vendor's merchandise returns over eighteen months. The audience can see at a glance the direction that returns are taking, even though the monthly percentage returns are scattered around.

Rule 7: Label Key Features of Your Graphs

Make sure that your audience will understand at a glance what the quantitative data in your graphs represent. For example, in the first graph of figure C-5, we see data for a particular company. But what does each column represent? Complaints per salesperson? Total sales revenues? District sales revenues? A month or a quarter of revenues?

FIGURE C-4

Percentage Returns

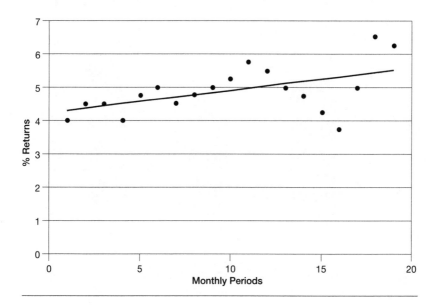

Are the values on the vertical axis dollars or thousands of dollars? Or are they euros?

Now look at a better-labeled version of the same chart in figure C-5. We can now see that each column represents the dollar value of Acme Company sales, expressed in thousands, for the first three months of 2003.

With the availability of graphics software, it has become easier and easier to prepare visual illustrations for any presentation you may make. Observe these seven rules for the use of graphics, and your presentations will be more professional and more effective.

FIGURE C-5

Unlabeled Versus Labeled Graph

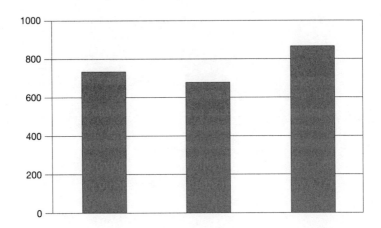

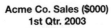

Acme Co. Sales ($000)
1st Qtr. 2003

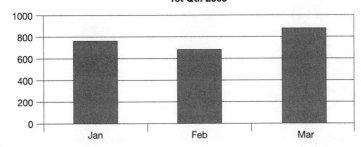

Notes

Chapter 1: Good Writing

1. William Strunk Jr., and E. B. White, *The Elements of Style*, 3rd ed. (New York: Macmillian, 1979), 23.

2. Nathaniel Hawthorne, *The House of the Seven Gables* (New York: Penguin Books), 5.

3. Ernest Hemingway, *For Whom the Bell Tolls* (New York, Charles Scribner's Sons, 1940), 471.

Chapter 2: Start-Up Strategies

1. The material in this section was adapted from Deborah Dumaine and the Better Communications® Team, *Instant-Answer Guide to Business Writing*, Lincoln, NE: Writers Club Press, 2003, and Deborah Dumaine and the Better Communications® Team, *Write to the Top: Writing for Corporate Success*, New York: Random House, 2004 (revised edition).

Chapter 3: The First Draft

1. This section was adapted from "Writing Clearly," part 2, "The Paragraph," *Harvard Management Communication Letter* (July 2000): 7–8.

2. Mary Munter, *Guide to Managerial Communication*, 5th ed. (Upper Saddle River, NJ: Prentice Hall, 2000), 52.

Chapter 4: Getting It Right

1. John S. Fielden, "What Do You Mean You Don't Like My Style?" *Harvard Business Review* (May–June 1982): 3.

2. Ibid., 5.

Chapter 5: Everyday Writing

1. The material in this section is adapted from Michael Hattersley, "Checklist for Preparing a Superior Memo," *Harvard Management Update* (February 1997).

2. Munter, *Guide to Managerial Communication*, 85–103.

3. This section on e-mail draws largely on Nick Morgan, "Don't Push That Send Button!" *Harvard Management Communication Letter* (August 2002): 9–11.

4. This section on e-mail policy is adapted from Steven Gossett, "How to Avoid E-Mail Lawsuits," *Harvard Management Communication Letter* (August 2000): 10–11.

Chapter 6: Presentations

1. The discussion of the Greek method of presentation draws largely on "Presentations and the Ancient Greeks," *Harvard Management Communication Letter* (January 1999): 5–8.

2. This section on the styles of learning is adapted from "Presentations That Appeal to All of Your Listeners," *Harvard Management Communication Letter* (June 2000): 4–5.

3. Shakespeare, *Henry V*, act 4, scene 3, lines 40–67.

Chapter 7: Backstage

1. This chapter is adapted directly from Harvard ManageMentor Module, "Making a Presentation," 15 December 2001, available at <http://harvardbusinessonline.hbsp.harvard.edu/b02/en/elearning/elearning_home.jhtml>.

Chapter 8: Show Time

The material in this chapter was adapted, except where noted, from Harvard ManageMentor Module, "Making a Presentation."

1. As cited in Nick Morgan, "How to Make Even Weak Speeches Great," *Harvard Management Communication Letter* (August 2001).

2. This section is adapted from Richard Bierck, "Are You Listening to Me?" *Harvard Management Communication Newsletter* (April 2001).

3. This section is adapted from Constantine Von Hoffman, Richard Bierck, Michael Hattersley, and Nick Wreden, "Handling Q&A: The Five Kinds of Listening," *Harvard Communication Update* 2 (February 1999).

Chapter 9: Dialogue

1. For a more complete description of catchball, see George Labovitz and Victor Rosansky, *The Power of Alignment* (New York: John Wiley and Sons, 1997), 90–92.

2. Paul Ekman, *Telling Lies: Clues to Deceit in the Marketplace, Politics, and Marriage* (New York: W. W. Norton, 1992), as described in "How Can You Tell When Your Teammate Is Lying?" *Harvard Management Communication Letter* (January 2000).

Appendix B: Writing the Perfect Job Application Cover Letter

1. Michael E. Hattersley, "Writing the Perfect Cover Letter," *Harvard Management Communication Letter* (October 1999).

Glossary

ACTIVE LISTENING giving one's respectful and undivided attention to both the words of a speaker and the emotions behind the spoken words, which are generally signaled through body language and vocal delivery.

ANTITHESIS a rhetorical device that places a sentence or one of its parts in opposition to another in order to capture the listener's attention or to evoke a strong response.

AUDITORY LEARNERS individuals whose primary learning style is more responsive to words and other sounds than to other stimuli.

BRAINSTORM OUTLINING a writing start-up strategy that uses free association to generate the ideas that will go into one's writing. In this strategy, the author jots down ideas as they come into his or her head. Those thoughts then become the bases for generating other ideas. All are then organized into an outline.

CATCHBALL a cross-functional method for accomplishing two things: idea enrichment/improvement, and buy-in among participants.

DESIGN ELEMENTS headings, subheadings, short blocks of text, graphics, and white space used to make a piece of written text less formidable, more comprehensible, and easier to skim.

EMPATHY the ability to identify with or vicariously experience the thoughts or feelings of others.

FREE WRITING METHOD a writing start-up strategy that relies on the author's freely roaming imagination. In this method, the author jots down anything that comes into his or her head. Once ideas stop flowing, the author highlights important ideas and organizes them into logical categories.

KINESTHETIC LEARNER an individual whose primary learning style is engaged by physical activities: handling a prototype, working at a laboratory bench, and so forth.

OUTLINING METHOD a writing start-up strategy that develops and organizes key points and subpoints into a nested structure that uses letters and roman and arabic numerals to indicate levels of information. Roman numbers identify the highest-level headings, with capital letter headings (A, B, C, etc.) nested under them. More details may be nested under those capital letter headings in the form of arabic numerals (1, 2, 3, etc.).

PARALLEL STRUCTURE a rhetorical device that uses sentence elements that are alike in both function and construction—for example, "We will work hard. We will work smart. We will not tire or fail."

QUESTIONING METHOD a writing start-up strategy that anticipates questions readers might have about the topic. By turning those questions into affirmative statements, the writer creates a list of points to be covered.

RHETORICAL QUESTION a question asked for the sole purpose of producing an effect on the audience. The speaker does not expect the question to be answered—least of all by the audience.

SCOPING a writing practice in which the author determines the breadth of the subject and how deeply it will be covered.

STYLE the choice of words, sentences, and paragraph format in a piece of writing that produces the desired reaction and result.

SUBJECT LINE in a memo or an e-mail, the part of the opening format through which the writer describes the general contents and aims to capture the reader's attention.

TRADITIONAL OUTLINING See *Outlining method*.

TRIAD a rhetorical device that uses a list of three items.

VISUAL LEARNER a person whose primary learning style responds best to pictures, graphs, and other visual stimuli.

For Further Reading

Dumaine, Deborah, and the Better Communications® Team. *Instant-Answer Guide to Business Writing*. Lincoln, NE: Writers Club Press, 2003. If you do lots of writing, this definitive reference work should be on your shelf. Organized alphabetically, it contains expert advice and examples on all points of grammar, punctuation, writing style, the use of presentation graphs, and much more.

Dumaine, Deborah, and the Better Communications® Team. *Write to the Top: Writing for Corporate Success*, New York: Random House, 2004 (revised edition). A time-saving, step-by-step approach to writing business documents that drive action.

Ekman, Paul. *Telling Lies: Clues to Deceit in the Marketplace, Politics, and Marriage*. New York: W. W. Norton, 1992. Ekman, one of the world's experts on this subject, reveals how to spot clues that what you're hearing is not the truth.

Fielden, John S. "What Do You Mean You Don't Like My Style?" *Harvard Business Review*, May–June 1982. The appropriate style of a written message varies with the purpose of the message and the relationship between the writer and the reader. This article explains how to determine the best style for many typical business situations. Though first published in 1982, the article remains timely and the best source on the subject. Reprints are available through Harvard Business Online at <www.hbsp.harvard.edu>.

Munter, Mary. *Guide to Managerial Communication*. 6th ed. Upper Saddle River, NJ: Prentice Hall, 2003. An excellent guide to effective business writing and speaking. The book contains a very good section on the use of visual aids.

Strunk, William Jr., E. B. White, and Roger Angell. *The Elements of Style*. 4th ed. Boston: Allyn and Bacon, 2000. This timeless little book, whose origins go back to the 1930s, has been the English language's most effective advocate for clear, concise, and more effective writing. Buy it. Read it. Follow its advice.

Index

active listening, 128–129, 130
antithesis use in presentations, 86
audience
   engaging during a presentation,
     110–112
   focusing on, 3–5
   as the subject of a paragraph,
     33–34
   testing a memo on, 67
   understanding for a presentation,
     97
auditory learners, 88, 89
authorship considerations, 11

bar and column charts, 147
brainstorm outline method, 22–25
broadcast letter, 142
business letters. *See also* cover
    letters
   format, 68–70
   goodwill factor, 70–72
   summary, 77
business writing
   drafts (*see* draft writing)
   e-mail (*see* e-mail)
   getting started (*see* start-up
     strategies for writing)
   letters (*see* business letters; cover
     letters)

memos (*see* memos)
   purposes of, 2–3
business writing principles
   audience focus, 3–5
   delivery strategy considerations,
     11–13
   economy of words, 8–9
   simple sentences use, 9–11
   statement of message, 6–7
   summary, 14–15
   topic focus, 6–8
   visual design, 38–41, 137

catchball, 128
colorful style use in writings,
    49–51
committees and business writing,
    6–7
cover letters. *See also* business
    letters
   argument creation, 140–141
   broadcast letter, 142
   guidelines, 139–140
   Me-You-We model, 141
   pronoun use, 142

delivering a presentation
   audience engagement, 110–112

delivering a presentation, *(continued)*
  evaluating a presentation, 118–119
  group presentations, 116–117
  question and answer session, 112–116
  speaking suggestions, 108–109
  stage fright and, 117–118
  summary, 119–120
design elements
  graphics use, 40–41
  guidelines, 137
  headings and subheadings, 38–39
  text block length, 39–40
dialogue essentials
  active listening, 128–129, 130
  catchball, 128
  detecting falsehoods, 129–131
  power as a mode of communication, 126–128
  summary, 131
  understanding others' perceptions, 123–126
  understanding the other person, 123–124
draft writing. *See also* start-up strategies for writing
  design elements, 38–41
  editing *(see under editing headings)*
  paragraph development, 32–36
  start-up strategy, 30–31
  summary, 41–42, 59
  transitions, 36–37

editing for accuracy, 56–59, 60, 136
editing for content
  beginning check, 44–45
  checklist, 136
  logic check for middle, 45–46
  summary, 59

  tips for endings, 46
  wrap-up effectiveness, 46–47
editing for sentence structure
  checklist, 136
  economy of words, 51–53
  jargon avoidance, 53–54
  quality of structure, 54–55
  sentence length, 55
  summary, 60
  voice, 55–56
editing for style
  checklist, 136
  colorful, 49–51
  forceful, 47–48
  impersonal, 48–49
  passive voice, 48
  personal, 48
  summary, 60
e-mail
  attachments, 75
  company policy elements, 76
  one message rule, 73–74
  potential problems, 72
  subject line content, 73
  summary, 77
  tips for, 74

falsehoods, detection in dialogues, 129–131
forceful style use in writings, 47–48
format considerations when writing, 12, 14
free writing method, 25–26

glossary, 153–154
goodwill factor, 70–72
graphics use in reports, 40–41, 137. *See also* visual aids
Greek speech model, 81–84. *See also* presentations

group presentations, 116–117

humor use in presentations, 111

impersonal style use in writings, 48–49

kinesthetic learners, 88, 89

letters. *See* business letters; cover letters
line charts, 147

media choices for presentations, 103
memos
  execution elements, 65–66
  format, 64
  purposes of and planning for, 62–64
  summary, 77
  testing against an audience, 67

one-on-one communication. *See* dialogue essentials
opening for a presentation, 99–100

paragraph development
  audience as subject, 33–34
  beginning and end, 32–33
  general statement as beginning, 35–36
  issue, point, discussion, 34–35
  number of subjects used, 33, 34
parallel structure in presentations, 85
personal style use in writings, 48
pie charts, 146–147
preparing a presentation
  content review, 98
  deciding what to say, 98–99

defining the objective, 96–97
media choices, 103
organization, 99–101
preliminary planning worksheet, 134
presentation outline, 135
rehearsing, 104–105
summary, 105–106
tips for adding interest, 101
understanding the audience, 97
visual aids guidelines, 101–104, 143–150
presentations
  argument introduction, 83
  conclusion, 84
  delivery (*see* delivering a presentation)
  emotional approach, 90–93
  five-part structure rationale, 81
  group, 116–117
  introduction suggestions, 81–82
  learning styles considerations, 88–89
  narrative use, 83
  preparing (*see* preparing a presentation)
  refutation, 84
  rhetorical devices, 85–87
  summary, 93

Q&A sessions in presentations
  anticipating questions, 112–114
  in group presentations, 117
  techniques for handling, 114–116
questioning method, 18–20

rhetorical questions use in presentations, 87

scattergrams, 147–148

sentence structure. *See* editing for sentence structure

stage fright, 117–118

start-up strategies for writing. *See also* draft writing
brainstorm outline method, 22–25
free writing method, 25–26
questioning method, 18–20
scoping a project, 26–27
summary, 27–28
traditional outline method, 20–21

style, writing. *See* editing for style

subject line content for e-mails, 73

timing considerations, 11–12

traditional outline method, 20–21

triad use in presentations, 85–86

visual aids
graphics use in reports, 40–41, 137
guidelines, 137, 143–150
in presentations, 101–104

visual learners, 88, 89

voice in writings, 47–48, 55–56

Wizards, 71

worksheets
editing checklist, 136
presentation outline, 135
presentation planning, 134
visual design, 137

About the Subject Adviser

Professor **MARY MUNTER** has taught management communication for over twenty-five years, for seven years at the Stanford Graduate School of Business and since 1983 at the Tuck School of Business at Dartmouth.

Professor Munter is considered one of the leaders in the management communication field. Among her publications is the *Guide to Managerial Communication*—recently published in its sixth edition and named "one of the five best business books" by the *Wall Street Journal*. She has also published many other articles and books and consulted with over ninety corporate and not-for-profit clients.

About the Writer

RICHARD LUECKE is the writer of several books in the Harvard Business Essentials series. Based in Salem, Massachusetts, Mr. Luecke has authored or developed over thirty books and dozens of articles on a wide range of business subjects. He has an M.B.A. from the University of St. Thomas.